Dwight D. Eisenhower

34th President of
the United States

Dwight Eisenhower became the 34th President of the United States in 1953. During his eight years in office, the World War II hero presided over a prosperous and peaceful nation. (Dwight D. Eisenhower Library; U.S. Navy.)

Dwight D. Eisenhower

34th President of the United States

Rafaela Ellis

 GARRETT EDUCATIONAL CORPORATION

Manufactured in the United States of America

Edited and produced by Synthegraphics Corporation

Library of Congress Cataloging in Publication Data

Ellis, Rafaela.
  Dwight D. Eisenhower, 34th president of the United States.
  (Presidents of the United States)
  Bibliography: p.
  Includes index.
  Summary: Presents a biography of the West Point graduate who served as Supreme Military Commander during World War II and as the thirty-fourth President of the United States.
  1. Eisenhower, Dwight D. (Dwight David),
1890–1969 — Juvenile literature. 2. Presidents — United States — Biography — Juvenile literature. [1. Eisenhower, Dwight D. (Dwight David), 1890–1969. 2. Presidents.]
I. Title. II. Title: Dwight D. Eisenhower, thirty-fourth president of the United States. III. Series.
E836.E45 1989   973.921'092'4 — dc19 [B] [92]
88-24538
ISBN 0-944483-13-5

Contents

Chronology for Dwight D. Eisenhower

1890 Born on October 14

1915 Graduated from West Point; assigned to Fort Sam Houston, Texas

1916 Married Mamie Geneva Doud on July 1

1917–1929 Served at American military bases in the United States and abroad

1929 Assigned to the office of the Assistant Secretary of War

1932 Appointed assistant to General Douglas MacArthur

1935–1939 Stationed in the Philippines with MacArthur

1939 Appointed to the General Staff of the U.S. War Department

1942 Appointed commander of the Allied invasion of North Africa

1944 Named Supreme Commander, Allied Expeditionary Force, for the invasion of Europe

1945–1948 Served as Chief of Staff of the U.S. Army

1948–1950 Served as president of Columbia University

1951–1953 Served as commander of NATO forces in Europe

1953–1961 Served as 34th President of the United States

1969 Died on March 28

Chapter 1

Storming the Beaches

In mid-1944, the forces of Adolf Hitler's Nazi Germany were firmly entrenched along the Normandy coast of France. World War II had been raging since 1939, when the Nazis had marched into Poland. After the Germans then conquered France in 1940, they continued their war of aggression throughout Europe and into Africa. Hitler then lost some territory in Italy and French North Africa in 1943, but as of mid-1944, he still held France — and much of Europe — firmly under his thumb.

It was clear to the Nazis that their enemies, the Allies (the combined forces of the United States, Great Britain, Canada, Australia, and freedom-fighters from many German-occupied nations), would mount a battle for control of Western Europe sometime in 1944. In December 1943, Hitler told his generals, "If they [the Allies] attack in the west, that attack will decide the war."

D-DAY: JUNE 6, 1944

Before dawn on June 6, 1944, a massive convoy of ships swept across the English Channel, steaming toward the Normandy beaches in France. Inside, tens of thousands of Allied soldiers, dressed in camouflage-green battle gear, prepared to take the Germans by surprise and storm Normandy's beaches. Back in England, thousands more soldiers and airmen climbed into fighter planes, awaiting orders to take off for the French coast.

As the morning light broke over the water, the ships came to rest along the French shore. Suddenly, they flung open their hatches, spilling thousands of soldiers onto the beaches. The men hit the shore running, firing at German troops in fortified bunkers. Then, before the Germans could realize what was happening, they saw huge tanks heading for shore after being dropped off by giant tank-carrying ships. Soon, bombers were screaming overhead, blasting the German positions to support the troops' movements on the ground.

Although many Allied soldiers fell victim to the German guns, the troops kept coming. Ships continued to drop men and supplies at the shore while planes dropped thousands of Allied paratroopers from the sky to set up communications posts and battle stations behind the German lines.

Operation Overlord

The Allied forces that invaded France on June 6, 1944, were part of the largest and most thoroughly planned military operation in the history of warfare. It involved 7,774 planes, 4,308 ships, and more than 3,000 tanks and other types of military vehicles. It also required more than 10 million ship-tons of supplies, and before it was over, more than 2.8 million officers, enlisted men, and staff personnel had participated in the event. This mighty invasion of western Europe, the code name of which was Operation Overlord, smashed the German army in France and, ultimately, led to the destruction of Adolf Hitler's Third Reich.

Operation Fortitude: Giving Away Secrets

Although Hitler had long suspected that the Allied invasion of Europe would come from the West, the Germans were not willing to rely on Hitler's instinct alone. To gain more reliable information about the Allies' plans, the Germans placed spies throughout Europe and Asia. In the spring of 1944, these agents reported a number of things that seemed to indicate an Allied attack in the near future.

In Great Britain, some of the German agents had seen huge military installations just across the English Channel from the province of Pas-de-Calais, France. From the air, German pilots saw fleets of airplanes and tanks on the ground, apparently preparing for an attack on Pas-de-Calais' shores. However, other German agents were equally convinced that the Allies would attack in southern Europe, because British General Bernard Montgomery had been seen touring the area along the Mediterranean Sea. Still other spies had intercepted radio communications indicating that the Allies were planning to launch an attack from Sweden.

This conflicting information thoroughly confused the Germans, and that's just what the Allies wanted. The German spies had fallen victim to Operation Fortitude, a plan designed to throw them off the trail of the real Allied invasion. The military installations that the German pilots had seen from the air were fakes—the planes and tanks were made

of papier-mâché. The man who had toured
the Mediterranean was not General Montgomery at all, but an actor who looked like
him. And the Allied messages that the Germans had intercepted were also fakes—
created expressly for the purpose of confus-
ing the enemy.

The Allies' real military bases were hidden
under camouflage, and General Montgomery
was in England, preparing his battle plans for
the invasion. The German agents had seen
only what the Allies had wanted them to see,
and it left Hitler's army thoroughly unprepared
for Operation Overlord when it finally
occurred.

In addition to the military personnel who participated
in the invasion itself, there were hundreds of thousands of
other people from all walks of life who were involved in the
planning and execution of Operation Overlord. But ultimately,
every detail of this largest operation in military history was
the responsibility of one man: General Dwight David Eisenhower, the Supreme Commander, Allied Expeditionary Force.
It was Eisenhower who was responsible for deciding the time
and place of the invasion, for allocating men and equipment
to it, and for giving the final order: "Go!"

If the Normandy landings were a success, Eisenhower
would receive the hero's mantle; but if it did not succeed,
he—and he alone—would bear the responsibility for failing
to crush Hitler's army. Hours before the invasion, Eisenhower
had scratched out a note that he would send to Franklin D.

Roosevelt, the President of the United States, if the attack failed: "Our landings in the Cherbourg-Havre area have failed to gain a satisfactory foothold and I have withdrawn the troops. . . . If any blame or fault attaches to the attempt, it is mine alone." Fortunately, Eisenhower never had to send that note. The six months of planning that he had devoted to the D-Day invasion paid off; within a few months, Hitler's army would be defeated.

THE MAN WHO LED THEM

The job of Supreme Commander was the biggest job in the biggest war the world had ever known. The man who held it, General Dwight David Eisenhower, was in many ways an unlikely candidate for the role. He had grown up poor on the Kansas plains and, as a young man, had once considered becoming a *gaucho* (cowboy) in Argentina.

Known to his men and to people around the world as "Ike," Eisenhower made an indelible mark on history and engraved his name into the hearts of millions. The D-Day invasion marked the beginning of the end for Hitler's reign of terror in Europe; it also marked a new beginning for Dwight Eisenhower. From that day forward, the Supreme Commander of the Allied Expeditionary Force would continue to find himself at the center of world events. And within a decade, as the nation's 34th President, he would become the Commander-in-Chief of the United States.

Chapter 2

An American Childhood

In 1741 a bearded German peasant boarded a creaking sailing ship for the long voyage to the New World. He was sailing toward a dream: a dream of sylvan vistas, fertile soil, and a new land—a land of freedom. He could not know, nor could he imagine, the momentous effect his trip would have on the history of the world.

That German peasant was Hans Nicholas Eisenhauer, great-great-great-grandfather of Dwight David Eisenhower. A little more than 200 years from the day that Hans Nicholas set out for his voyage, his descendant would lead the armies of the Free World to victory against the mighty forces of the German fatherland, and would go on to become the 34th President of the United States.

A CHILDHOOD ON THE PRAIRIE

Dwight David Eisenhower was born in Denison, Texas, on October 14, 1890. He was born into a big family that included his parents, Ida and David, and three older brothers, Arthur, Edgar, and Roy. Within a few years, two more brothers—Milton and Earl—would round out the Eisenhower clan.

Dwight's father, David Jacob Eisenhower, was the son of a farmer from Kansas. In 1884, David enrolled in college at Lane University in Lecompton, Kansas, where he later met Ida Stover, a former schoolteacher. The young couple were married a year after they met and settled in the small town of Abilene, Kansas, where David and a partner opened a general store. Because Kansas was in the middle of a terrible drought at that time, many of the local farmers had little money. So, although the store had plenty of customers, few of them could afford to pay their bills. David Eisenhower generously let the farmers buy on credit, and within three years the store was bankrupt. David's unscrupulous business partner ran off with what little cash remained, leaving David completely broke.

In search of a way to provide for his family, David moved to Denison, Texas, where he took a job as a railroad worker. After he had saved up enough cash, he sent for his wife and three sons. In 1890, soon after the family had settled in Denison, the Eisenhowers welcomed their fourth son – Dwight.

When Dwight was less than a year old, the Eisenhowers moved back to Abilene, where David took a job as an engineer in the Belle Springs Creamery. It was in this tiny Kansas farm town that the future President grew up.

Life in a Small Town

Dwight Eisenhower once said that his childhood was much like those of millions of youngsters growing up in small-town America at the turn of the century. His parents were very religious and taught their sons the basic values of hard work, fair play, and respect for others and for God.

Although money was scarce, David and Ida Eisenhower managed to provide a happy childhood for their sons. Ida

"Little Ike" (front row, second from left) attended the Lincoln School in Abilene. His farmer's overalls contrasted sharply with the finer clothes of his classmates. (Dwight D. Eisenhower Library.)

made sure that her boys were well fed and had clean clothes to wear, and David made sure that his sons grew up knowing the value of an education. David himself took correspondence courses to help him in his work at the Belle Springs Creamery.

The Eisenhower boys were no strangers to labor. They were expected to help their mother with the household chores, to feed the few chickens and cows that the family kept, and to clean out the stable behind the house. (They knew that if they didn't, their father would not spare the rod.) None of the boys ever received an allowance; instead, David gave each of them a small plot of land behind the house where they could raise crops to earn spending money. Dwight raised corn and used the money he earned to buy clothes, football equipment, and a rifle.

School Days

In 1896 young Dwight Eisenhower entered Lincoln School, where he became known as "Little Ike," short for "Little Eisenhower" (his older brother, Edgar, was known as "Big Ike"). Soon, however, Dwight's nickname was shortened to "Ike."

Blond, blue-eyed Ike was a scrappy, energetic boy. Although only a fair student, he was excellent in reading because he had to read the Bible at home. By his own admission, however, his "conduct was not the equal of [his] reading ability," for he was always getting into scrapes. For one thing, he never shied away from a fight. The Eisenhowers lived on the "wrong side of the tracks" in Abilene—literally. The train tracks that separated the wealthy north side of the town from the working-class south side ran right in front of their house. Ike spent a lot of his recesses wrestling in the schoolyard with "uppity" north-siders who made fun of his hand-me-down clothes and worn-out shoes.

A Young Adventurer

The thing that got young Ike into the most trouble, both at school and at home, was his love of adventure. Once, when a flood swept through Abilene, Ike and one of his brothers "set out to explore." They found a piece of floating sidewalk and turned it into a raft on which they floated down the swollen streets of Abilene, much like Huck Finn on the Mississippi River. Laughing as they glided down the flooded street, the boys failed to notice that they were heading straight for the raging waters of the river. If a concerned neighbor hadn't forced them to turn back, they probably would have drowned. When they got home, soaked to the skin, Ike and his brother were met by their angry father, who taught them a lesson with a hickory switch.

Another adventure had far more serious results. When he was a freshman at Abilene High School, Ike fell on his knee while sliding down a wooden platform with some friends. Two days later, the leg became infected. In those days, there were no drugs to fight infection, and Ike "dropped off . . . into delirium," hovering near death for several weeks. The doctor thought that the only way to stop the infection was to amputate Ike's leg.

Although he was floating in and out of consciousness, Ike managed to overhear the doctor's plan and was horrified. He told his brother Edgar that he would rather die than be without a leg and not be able to play football. To stop the doctor from going through with his plan, Edgar slept in front of the door to Ike's room so that the doctor could not get in to perform the operation. Miraculously, Ike's stubborness paid off; in a few weeks the infection receded, and his leg was saved. But he was forced to stay out of school for the rest of the spring and ended up having to repeat his freshman year.

Activities at Abilene High

When he returned to Abilene High, Ike was finally able to indulge in his greatest passion – sports. He played both football and baseball, and played them well. But football was the sport he loved most, and he was one of the stars on the varsity team. In those days, however, schools did not provide money for sports. Students who wanted to play on a team had to supply their own uniforms, balls, and other items. Because Ike came from a poor family, he knew how hard it was for some students to pay for sports equipment. So he and a few friends formed the Abilene High School Athletic Association. For 25 cents a month, students could join the organization and help pay for sports gear. In his senior year, Ike was elected president of the association.

Ike also tried his hand at acting when he was in high school. He starred in Abilene High's senior play, a take-off of Shakespeare's *The Merchant of Venice.* Playing the comic character Launcelot Gobo, with red powder in his hair and black gum on his teeth to make him look toothless, Ike stole the show. The local newspaper said that Ike "won plenty of applause and deserved it. He . . . gave an impression that many professional [actors] fail to reach."

Despite his theatrical success, Ike was not interested in pursuing an acting career. He had only one goal: to go to college. But unfortunately, the entire family – Ike and his brothers included – had already used all their savings to send Ike's older brother, Edgar, to college. So after his graduation from high school on May 23, 1909, Ike immediately went to work, holding a number of odd jobs and saving every penny he earned toward his own college education.

COLLEGE AT LAST

In 1910, Ike was working in the icehouse of the same creamery where his father worked. His schedule was a rough one—he worked seven days a week, 12 hours a day. Still, he was not able to save enough money to go to college.

Then one day Ike heard of a way to go to college for free. A friend told him that a young man could get a free education at one of the two U.S. military academies—West Point for the Army and Annapolis for the Navy—if he served for a time in the military upon graduation. Ike immediately recognized that if he was going to get into college while he was still in his twenties, he would have to try for one of the military academies.

But getting admitted to either academy was not so easy. Both schools had difficult entrance exams. Furthermore, a young man could not simply apply as he could to an ordinary college; he had to be appointed on the recommendation of a member of Congress. Although he knew that his chances of being admitted were slim, Ike was determined to win an appointment to one of the schools.

Making the Grade

To ensure that he passed the entrance exams, Ike went back to high school for a series of refresher courses in his weakest subjects. Although he was working 12 hours a day, he studied every spare moment, sometimes getting less than four hours of sleep at night. But he knew that all his studying would not help him if he could not obtain a congressional recommendation.

Ike wrote to Kansas Senator Joseph Bristow, requesting an appointment to one of the military academies. His application to Senator Bristow was reinforced by letters of support from many of Abilene's leading citizens, who assured the senator that young Dwight Eisenhower was a hard worker who would make a fine addition to the United States armed forces.

In the summer of 1910, Ike took the entrance exam for Annapolis. Although he felt he had done well, he would have to wait weeks for the results. While he was waiting, he received some devastating news: applicants for Annapolis had to be between the ages of 16 and 20 at the time of admission. Because he had been forced to go to work directly out of high school, Ike would be 21 by the time the next class entered Annapolis. He was disqualified; his hopes were dashed.

Hope Rekindled

When he found out that he could not get into Annapolis, Ike was heartbroken. He envisioned himself working for years at the creamery before he could save up enough money to be able to go to college. Many times he almost gave up hope, but he was determined to keep trying. Then he learned that, unlike Annapolis, West Point had no age requirement for its entrants. His hope renewed, Ike decided to try for West Point. He continued to study, and asked Senator Bristow to recommend him for the Army academy. Early in 1911 Ike received the news – he had been accepted to West Point, conditional on his passing the entrance exams.

His intensive studying for Annapolis had prepared Ike well, and he easily passed the West Point exams, including a battery of physical and psychological tests. On June 14, 1911, Dwight David Eisenhower reported to the United States Military Academy at West Point, New York, to join the class of 1915.

Chapter 3

The West Point Experience

On a hot June morning in 1911, Dwight David Eisenhower hugged his weeping mother, shook hands with his father, and walked down a dusty street to the Abilene train station. With nothing but a cardboard suitcase in his hand and a five-dollar bill in his pocket, he boarded a train for West Point. The train trip took three days, but it set Eisenhower on a half-century journey that resulted in one of history's greatest military careers and, ultimately, the American presidency.

Ike was a lot like the other young men in West Point's class of 1915. Good-looking and smart, he personified the college man of his day. In other ways, however, there was a world of difference between Ike and his classmates. Many of them were from wealthy families who had a tradition of attending West Point. When he arrived at the academy, Ike felt like "a gawky Kansas boy from the farm country," lost in a sea of more sophisticated young men.

LIFE AT THE POINT

Although he was a bit intimidated at first, Ike quickly adjusted to West Point. Still, his first few months there were not without some setbacks. His first day seemed to him "one of calculated chaos." New cadets were given the "West Point treatment" from the moment they arrived. The faculty greeted the cadets with nonstop shouting: "Suck in that stomach! Shoulders back! Hurry up! Hurry up!" For Ike, the pace seemed relentless. "No one was allowed to do anything at ordinary quick-time; everything was on the double," he later remembered.

A Plebe's Life

First-year cadets, called "plebes," had to take orders from both the faculty and older students, known as "yearlings." The yearlings took great pleasure in "crawling," or hazing, the plebes. Some favorite crawling orders included forcing a plebe to pick up all the ants in an anthill one by one or to do 100 push-ups on command. The yearlings also called the plebes insulting names, such as "Mr. Dumgard" or "Mr. Dumbjohn."

Some plebes could not handle the constant harassment. Ike's first roommate cried himself to sleep every night for a month, and eventually resigned. Many others followed him in quitting West Point. Of the 265 cadets who entered with Eisenhower in 1911, only 164 graduated four years later. Many, like the great writer Edgar Allan Poe (who entered West Point in 1830), found the academy a "God-forsaken place."

Ike, however, enjoyed poking fun at West Point's rules. Once, when a yearling ordered him to report to his quarters in "full dress coats" (military code for complete formal dress),

Ike showed up in his coat alone—without another stitch of clothing on him. This ability to laugh at the rigid rules helped him survive the first uncomfortable months at the Point.

Still, Ike did find West Point trying at times. For one thing, he had a hard time learning all the endless rules and regulations that the academy imposed. He also had a problem figuring out who to salute. He once saluted the band's drum major because he assumed that someone with so many medals on his uniform must be an officer. He even found it hard to master all the physical requirements of the academy. Learning to march was "more than difficult," and Ike was assigned to the "Awkward Squad" until he could get it right.

A Rebel in Uniform

Ike's greatest trouble at the Point was his constant desire to break the rules. Because he loved to flout authority, Ike was better known for his demerits at West Point than for his leadership.

Ike received demerits for everything, and he often worked hard to get them. When he learned that cadets were allowed to smoke only pipes or cigars, he began rolling his own cigarettes and smoking them in the hallways, in plain view of his superiors. After an officer at an academy dance scolded him for dancing too wildly with a young lady, Ike did the same step—with the same young lady—at the next dance. And even though he knew how important punctuality was at the Point, Ike was frequently late to class.

The punishment for amassing too many demerits was the grueling assignment of "walking the arena"—that is, marching up and down the West Point Arena for one hour a day for a certain number of weeks for each excessive demerit.

Ike (third from left) was one of the most active and popular
cadets in the West Point class of 1915. Although he enjoyed
breaking the rules, Eisenhower also believed in doing his duty.
As a member of the Color Guard, he carried the West Point
flag at academy ceremonies. (Dwight D. Eisenhower Library.)

Ike walked the arena constantly while he was at the Point.
Ultimately, his many demerits resulted in a change in academy
policy toward walking the arena. After Ike got out of walking off his demerits because he was in the hospital during
the period he was suppose to be walking the arena, the
academy decided that demerit holders should be assigned to
walk only a certain number of hours, not weeks.

THE SCHOLAR-ATHLETE

As he had been at Abilene High, Ike was a good student at West Point. An excellent writer, he did well in English, and he was good enough in calculus to once tell his professor how to correctly solve a problem (Ike's unique shortcut was later incorporated into the curriculum). But the area in which Ike excelled the most in his early years at the Point was the one he loved the most – sports.

"It would be difficult to overemphasize the importance that I attached to participation in sports," Ike later wrote. As in high school, sports became the center of Ike's world at West Point. He excelled in baseball, and his coach told him that he was a good prospect for the sophomore team. But his real ambition was to play football. In his freshman year, Ike tried out for the Cullum Hall, or junior varsity, football team and made it. By the fall of his second year, he was playing so well that he was promoted to the varsity team.

On the Football Field

Football provided Ike with some of the most exciting – and most painful – moments of his West Point career. He put his heart and soul into every game, and it paid off. He earned a varsity letter, played against such football "greats" as Olympic hero Jim Thorpe (whom Ike tackled during a game between West Point and the Carlisle Indian School), and even got the chance to read about himself in *The New York Times,* which called him "one of the most promising backs in Eastern football" in the fall of 1912.

Ike was tough on the field, and many opposing players found him downright scary. One rival found Ike so frightening that in the middle of a scrimmage he pointed at Ike and shouted to the referee, "Watch that man!" The referee responded, "Why? Has he slugged you or roughed you up?" "No," said the player, "But he's *going* to!"

A Serious Injury

Unfortunately for Ike, his brilliant football career was short-lived. During his second varsity season, one week before the annual Army-Navy game—the most important game of the year—Ike twisted his leg in a game against Tufts College. He had to be carried off the field and was immediately sent to the hospital.

For three days Ike lay in a hospital bed with a badly swollen knee. On the third day, however, the swelling went down, so Ike went back to football practice and military training. But a few days later, during a cavalry drill, Ike leapt off his horse to vault over it as it jumped a hurdle. When Ike landed, he heard a loud "pop." He knew right away that he had injured his leg again.

This time, Ike knew immediately that the injury was serious. The doctors spent four days straightening his leg, then they put it in a cast. Finally, the doctors gave Ike the bad news: he would never play football again.

No Reason to Live

When he heard that he could no longer play football, Ike was devastated. He saw no reason to go on living and quickly lost interest in everything. His grades went down, he stopped playing cards and joking with his friends, and he even stopped getting into trouble. Several times he thought of quitting West Point altogether. "Seems like I'm never cheerful anymore," he wrote to a friend in Abilene. "The fellows that used to call me 'Sunny Jim' call me 'Gloomy Face' now." Only the constant encouragement of his friends and classmates kept him from leaving the Point.

After a few months, however, Ike pulled himself together. At the request of a faculty member he became a coach for the junior varsity football team, which kept him in touch with football and lifted his spirits. He also became the varsity team's biggest cheerleader, traveling to all the games and shouting encouragement from the sidelines. Although he never got over the heartache caused by the abrupt end to his football career, Ike did not allow it to destroy his West Point career.

A COMMISSIONED OFFICER

On June 12, 1915, Dwight David Eisenhower graduated from West Point as a commissioned second lieutenant in the U.S. Army. Out of a class of 164, he placed 61st in academic rank and 125th in disciplinary rank (all those demerits added up). Because he had not yet received orders about his first Army assignment, he returned to Abilene for a vacation with his family.

Before he graduated, Ike was called to the office of the academy doctor for a conference. The doctor told Ike that his leg injury concerned the Army, and therefore the doctor did not know if he could recommend Ike for a commission.

If the doctor was expecting an argument from this about-to-graduate young cadet, he didn't get one. Instead, Ike said it was fine with him if he was not accepted into the Army—

he had always wanted to travel to South America anyway, and now he would have the freedom to do it.

That was all the doctor needed to hear. He decided that a man who wanted out of the Army that much must be kept in. He told Ike that he would recommend him for commission, provided Ike did not select too hazardous an assignment.

Once South America was out, Ike decided to choose an equally warm and exotic place for his first assignment. When asked where he would like to be stationed, he chose the Philippines, which at the time was a possession of the United States. Because few West Pointers shared Ike's enthusiasm for the tropics, he was sure he would get his assignment—so sure, in fact, that he spent his entire clothing allowance on tropical uniforms made of white linen and khaki.

But when Ike finally received his orders, he broke into one of his famous sheepish grins. Although he had spent his entire clothing allowance on tropical uniforms, he had been assigned to Fort Sam Houston, Texas, where he would need only olive drabs and dress blues. Fortunately, a tailor in Leavenworth, Kansas, gave Ike credit so he could buy the uniforms he needed. He was now outfitted for the United States Army.

Chapter 4

An Officer and a Gentleman

In September 1915, wearing one of the new uniforms he bought on credit, Second Lieutenant Dwight David Eisenhower reported to Fort Sam Houston, in San Antonio, Texas. There he joined the 19th Infantry Regiment of the United States Army.

FORT SAM HOUSTON

After enduring the rigors of West Point, Eisenhower found life at Fort Sam Houston quite relaxing. Because the United States was at peace, the young officer's assignments consisted mostly of administrative duties and training exercises. The pace was almost leisurely, and Ike could usually complete his official duties by noon. He would then spend the afternoons coaching football at a local military academy; his evenings were devoted to hunting, horseback riding, and playing poker.

Boy Meets Girl

It wasn't long before Eisenhower found another evening pursuit—romance. In October 1915, a fellow officer's wife introduced Ike to a striking young lady—Mamie Geneva Doud. Her family was from Denver, Colorado, but spent their winters in San Antonio. The 25-year-old officer was swept off his feet by the 19-year-old beauty. Mamie later noted that she thought Ike was "just about the handsomest male I [had] ever seen." For his part, Ike found Mamie "vivacious and attractive," with a "saucy" look in her eye.

Later on the evening they met, Ike phoned Miss Doud to ask her for a date on the following Saturday night. She claimed to be busy. "What about Sunday?" he asked. Again, she was busy. He named night after night; each time, the young lady responded that she was sorry, but she had another engagement that evening. Finally, Eisenhower named a date more than a month away. "Oh," Mamie said, "I have no plans for that evening. I'd love to see you."

Mamie later admitted that she was "playing hard to get," and it worked. After their first date, the couple began seeing one another almost every evening. On Valentine's Day 1916, only four months after their first date, Ike proposed. On July 1, 1916, Ike and Mamie were married.

Ike believed that an Army wife should make her husband the center of her world, and Mamie did not disappoint him. She quickly became the perfect Army wife. She learned all she could about the way the Army worked and made friends with other Army wives. She entertained Ike's fellow officers at frequent and lively parties, and soon the apartment she and Ike shared became known as "Club Eisenhower." Most importantly, she never complained—even though, during the first 35 years of their marriage, she and Ike moved 35 times.

Second Lieutenant Eisenhower married Mamie Geneva Doud five months after being introduced to her by a fellow officer's wife. The couple enjoyed 53 years of marriage. (Dwight D. Eisenhower Library.)

Ike taught Mamie about military strategy and the out-doors; Mamie taught Ike the social graces. A finishing-school graduate from a wealthy family, Mamie added a touch of refinement to the rough-and-ready Kansan.

WORLD WAR I

After their marriage, Ike and Mamie became an important part of the Fort Sam Houston social scene. But their blissful existence in Texas was short-lived. When the United States entered World War I in 1917, the Army began to mobilize. Ike was promoted to captain and made part of the 57th Infantry, an offshoot of the 19th Infantry that he had joined in 1915. He was sent to Fort Oglethorpe, Georgia, to teach officer candidates.

Fort Oglethorpe

For many reasons, life at Fort Oglethorpe was not very happy for Eisenhower. Because there were no accommodations for wives at the camp, Mamie returned to Denver to live with her family, and Ike missed her terribly. Also, Eisenhower wanted to go overseas and see war action, not stay at home and train recruits. But one good thing did happen while Ike was stationed at Oglethorpe: he received a telegram telling him that Mamie had given birth to their first child – Doud Dwight Eisenhower, whom Mamie nicknamed "Icky."

It would be several months before Ike could see his son. From Oglethorpe he was sent to Fort Leavenworth, Kansas, and from there to Camp Meade, Maryland, to command a tank battalion. Eisenhower was thrilled – he would soon be going overseas as the leader of a tank corps. But two days before he was to leave, his orders were changed. Although his battalion was sent to Europe, Ike was assigned to Camp Colt, Pennsylvania, to train another tank group.

Camp Colt

Eisenhower's disappointment at being denied an overseas assignment only deepened when he arrived at Camp Colt. Unused since the Civil War, the broken-down camp had few buildings, and the men had to spend the cold winter in tents while they rebuilt the camp and trained for war. Eisenhower's frustration was lessened, however, when he was able to rent a nearby house for Mamie and his young son to live in.

The whole time he was at Camp Colt, Eisenhower kept writing to the War Department requesting an overseas assignment. Finally, his wish was granted—he and his tank group would go to Europe in November 1918. Unfortunately for Eisenhower—but happily for the rest of the world—the armistice agreement ending World War I was signed on November 11. Eisenhower never got to Europe.

THE PEACETIME ARMY

After the war ended, the Army quickly demobilized. Thousands of men returned to civilian life, leaving the Army a skeleton of its former self. Eisenhower, who had been appointed a temporary lieutenant colonel during the war, reverted to the rank of permanent major.

In the autumn of 1919 Eisenhower was sent back to Camp Meade, Maryland, where he was again assigned to train tank crews. His duty this time was to help create the Infantry Tank School. The man who was assigned to assist him was George S. Patton, Jr., a West Point classmate.

Patton and Eisenhower became good friends. Eisenhower respected Patton because he had seen battle during World War I; the tough-talking Patton admired Eisenhower's quiet strength. Both were enthusiastic about testing tanks for use in battle. But tanks were a new weapon, and testing them could be dangerous. Once, during a testing exercise, a cable broke on one of the tanks, causing the huge machine to veer out of control. As the wayward tank barrelled toward them, Patton and Eisenhower had to dive into a ditch to avoid being crushed.

A Family Tragedy

One of the benefits of Camp Meade was that it had family quarters for married officers. Ike, Mamie, and Icky moved into a new home and immediately established another "Club Eisenhower." They became popular members of the base, enjoying an active social life.

In the winter of 1920, as the Eisenhowers prepared for a festive Christmas, Icky suddenly became ill. A doctor determined that the child had scarlet fever, which he had caught from the Eisenhowers' maid. For a week, Icky lay in a hospital bed while his father watched him through a window, praying for his recovery. Unfortunately, the prayers were in vain. In early January 1921, Icky died.

Ike and Mamie were devastated by Icky's death, and their tragedy was felt deeply by many other members of the camp. Icky had been a sort of camp mascot, and even had a small uniform that he wore to camp occasions. When the Eisenhowers left the base to carry Icky's body back to Denver for burial, the entire camp turned out to pay their respects to the young boy.

For the next year, the Eisenhowers grieved terribly. In January 1922, they finally got some relief when they were sent to the Panama Canal Zone. Although Mamie complained that their house in Panama was little more than a shack, and although the heat, the lizards, and the insects took some getting used to, the exotic atmosphere restored the young couple. Their recovery was made almost complete by the birth of a second son, John, in 1922.

In 1925, Major Eisenhower returned to Abilene for a reunion with his parents and five brothers. This portrait of the family on their front porch is the last picture ever taken of David and Ida Eisenhower with all of their sons. (Dwight D. Eisenhower Library.)

Life as a Major

During the next 18 years, Major Eisenhower and his family traveled from one military base to another. In 1924 they returned to the United States from Panama so that Eisenhower could attend the Army's Command and General Staff School in Leavenworth, Kansas. Although an aide to the Chief of Infantry had told Ike that "you will probably fail," he graduated first in a class of 275 students.

From there it was on to Washington, D.C., where Eisenhower was appointed to the Battle Monuments Commission. His assignment was to write a guide to American battlefields in Europe, and his superior officer on the project was the legendary World War I hero, General John J. "Blackjack" Pershing.

Eisenhower found Pershing cold and distant, and he was not sure that the great general liked him very much. But Pershing was so pleased with Eisenhower's work on the battlefield guide that he later asked Ike to help him write his memoirs. Although Pershing disregarded most of Eisenhower's advice, he appreciated it. As a reward, he sent Eisenhower to the Army War College at Fort McNair. This was a great honor, because McNair was where officers went to prepare for a high command.

Because the War College was located in Washington, the Eisenhowers did not have to move. Both Ike and Mamie were relieved, because they were having a grand time in the nation's capital. Mamie loved the social scene, and Ike enjoyed being close to his brother, Milton, an important official in the Department of Agriculture who had an apartment in the same building as Ike and Mamie. Soon, as they had done everywhere else they had ever lived, Ike and Mamie turned their Washington home into another "Club Eisenhower."

In 1928, when Eisenhower graduated from the War College, he was given a choice: he could go to France with the Battle Monuments Commission, or he could join the office of the General Staff of the War Department. Ike wanted to join the General Staff because such a position would enhance his career and allow him to work with some of the most important men in the Army. But Mamie had other ideas. For the first time in their marriage, she put her foot down: she wanted to go to Paris, and that was that. Ike gave in, and in August 1928 the Eisenhowers set out for France.

Paris provided the Eisenhowers with one of the most peaceful and enjoyable periods of their Army career. Young John was able to attend an American school, where he made many friends. "Club Eisenhower" was soon in full swing, becoming the center of social life for American officers and their wives. Mamie loved to shop in the chic boutiques, and Ike enjoyed roaming the battlefields of the war he had missed.

Back in the States

After 15 months in Paris, the Eisenhowers were sent back to Washington, where Ike was assigned to the office of the Assistant Secretary of War. He held this job until 1933, when he became the assistant to the Army Chief of Staff, General Douglas MacArthur.

This was a plumb assignment, and Eisenhower learned a lot. He was able to attend congressional hearings, to confer with officials in the various Cabinet departments, and to learn how the government really worked. Most important, he had the chance to learn from one of the greatest Army men of the day, General MacArthur.

In 1935, when General MacArthur was sent to the Philippines, he ordered Eisenhower to come with him. Although Ike had requested an assignment to the Philippines 20 years earlier, when he graduated from West Point, he was not happy about his new assignment. After years in administrative posts, he was looking forward to a chance to command troops. But General MacArthur was not a man who took "No" for an answer. Dwight Eisenhower headed for Manila.

In the Philippines

The Philippines was in a process of great change when Eisenhower arrived there in 1935. Formerly a possession of the United States, its status had been changed to that of a Commonwealth, and it was preparing for complete independence. The job MacArthur and his staff had to do was to see that the transition went smoothly.

Eisenhower's assignment was to create and train a Philippine defense force (although the United States intended to continue supporting the islands, it felt that the Filipinos should provide the bulk of their own defense). Toward this end, Eisenhower and a West Point classmate, Major James Ord, worked to form a Philippine air force. In the process, Eisenhower learned how to fly and later obtained his pilot's license.

Eventually, Mamie and John joined Ike in the Philippines, where the family lived until 1940. Then, as World War II raged in Europe, the Army decided that Eisenhower was needed elsewhere. In February 1940, he received orders to report to Fort Lewis, Washington.

Back Home Again

Mamie and Ike were thrilled to be back home; they reveled in the sights and sounds of America. Ike was happy because he was now in charge of training troops for combat. Mamie, always the perfect Army wife, was happy because her husband was happy.

Their joy was compounded in the summer of 1941 by

several events. First, Eisenhower was appointed Chief of Staff of the Third Army, which was headquartered at Fort Sam Houston. Second, he was promoted to the rank of full colonel, which had long been his highest aspiration in the Army. Third, he and Mamie celebrated 25 years of marriage. Finally, John had entered the freshman class at West Point, following in his father's footsteps. The appointment, Eisenhower beamed, "added two inches to my chest and volumes to Mamie's daily conversations about 'her son.' "

From August to September Ike led the Third Army in field maneuvers in Louisiana. Although it was one of the toughest assignments he ever had, he loved it. Slogging through the swamps with his troops, snatching a few moments of sleep under a tree, and all in all thoroughly tired, hot, and dirty, Ike for the first time felt like a commander of troops.

The maneuvers were the largest the Army had ever held, and for Ike they were a resounding success. His Third Army did so well that *The New York Times* praised Eisenhower by name, giving him complete credit for the efficiency of his men. (Unfortunately, they spelled his name wrong, referring to him as "Colonel D. D. Ersenbeen.") As usual, Ike claimed that he did not deserve the praise, but he was secretly overjoyed at the success of the operation. He was even more thrilled when he was made a temporary brigadier general as a result of his success.

As 1941 drew to a close, Dwight Eisenhower felt confident about his own future and that of his country. Although he was sure that the United States was bound to somehow become involved in the war in Europe, the maneuvers had given him confidence in America's ability to meet the challenge.

Chapter 5

The World at War

On the afternoon of December 7, 1941, Dwight Eisenhower laid down in his Fort Sam Houston office for a well-deserved nap. He had been working hard, and he told his assistant that he did not want to be disturbed for any reason. About an hour later, however, an aide rushed into Eisenhower's room and shook the commander out of his sleep. Before the startled Eisenhower could get a reprimand out of his mouth, the aide spoke. "The Japanese have just bombed the U.S. fleet at Pearl Harbor, Hawaii, sir," he said. "The United States is now at war."

Eisenhower was not completely unprepared for the events of December 1941. World War II had been raging in Europe for two years, ever since Nazi Germany, under the command of Adolf Hitler, had marched into Poland in late 1939. The Nazis had continued their march through Europe, taking over everything that lay in their path and rounding up millions of Jews, Poles, and anti-Nazis and sending them to concentration camps, where they were tortured and murdered. France had fallen to Hitler's army in the summer of 1940, and England had already suffered huge losses to the Axis powers (the name for the combined armies of Germany and its allies, most notably Italy).

What Eisenhower had not anticipated was the suddenness of America's involvement. He had long expected that the United States would somehow become embroiled in the fight in Europe, but while the nation was looking to Western Europe, war had come from the East. And as soon as the United States responded to Pearl Harbor by declaring war on Japan, Germany and Italy declared war on the United States. Almost overnight, the United States had been thrust into a global conflict.

A WARTIME LEADER

When the war began, Eisenhower had been in the Army for 25 years. He had spent 16 of those years as a major and had recently been promoted to full colonel, then to temporary brigadier general. He had commanded entire military bases, worked with Congress, and served as "right-hand man" to several of the most important generals of his time. He was a graduate of one of the nation's most prestigious military academies, and had attended—and excelled at—many of the Army's postgraduate facilities.

For all his experience, however, Eisenhower was not a famous military man. Unlike the men under whom he had served—especially Douglas MacArthur—he was virtually unknown to the public. He was like many of his West Point classmates: he had accomplished a lot but was still a rather obscure Army officer. But all that changed when Japanese bombs exploded on Hawaiian beaches on that sunny December day in 1941.

Service in the War Department

A week after Pearl Harbor, Eisenhower was summoned to Washington, D.C., by General George C. Marshall, the Army Chief of Staff. Marshall placed Eisenhower in charge of formulating a military policy for the Philippines, which were then under Japanese attack. Ike quickly went to work and soon created a plan that impressed Marshall. Thus began one of the most important relationships of Eisenhower's career.

In March of 1942 Marshall named Eisenhower commanding officer of the Operations Division of the War Department and promoted him to the temporary rank of major general. By the beginning of April, Eisenhower was in charge of a staff of 107 officers.

His new assignment was challenging and difficult, but Ike responded to it with skill and efficiency. Some of his techniques were innovative as well as practical. For example, he wired his entire office with Dictaphone machines. At the end of each day, secretaries would type up the recordings, providing Eisenhower with a detailed report of all the day's proceedings.

But even with these efficient methods, Ike worked at his desk for upwards of 16 hours a day. So busy was Eisenhower that he could not even return to Abilene when his father died in the spring of 1942. As Ike wrote in his diary, "War . . . has no time to indulge even the deepest and most sacred emotions."

Overseas to London

Eisenhower's goal in Washington was simply to do the best job he could, but the result of his efforts was much more. In June 1942 General Marshall appointed Ike commander of all American troops in England. With the stroke of a pen, Eisenhower became one of the most important officers in the U.S. Army.

Although Ike's title was impressive, it meant little to those outside the military. When his plane emerged from the fog to land outside London on June 24, he was met by nothing more than a little drizzle and a few staff officers. It was, however, the last time his movements would go unnoticed. The next day he held a press conference at which he identified himself as the new American commander. Suddenly, the flashbulbs popped and Dwight Eisenhower was world news. His grinning face appeared on the front page of newspapers around the globe. In an instant, he was transformed from an unknown staff officer into a major world figure. Back home, Mamie found herself a celebrity as well. The editor of almost every magazine in America wanted a story on the general's wife.

Working with the British

As popular as Eisenhower was with the press and the American people, he had a hard time getting the British to trust him. Many Britons were upset by the large number of American troops in their country in 1942. The way they saw it, England had been fighting Hitler virtually alone for years, and now the bragging, swaggering Americans had come in at the last minute to take over.

Compounding the problem was the unprofessional behavior of many American soldiers stationed in and around London. Most of these young men were poorly trained; many were downright rude. Far away from home and well paid by British standards, the Americans enjoyed spending their pay in London's many pubs—and on London's many young ladies. As one saying went, "The trouble with the Yanks [Americans] is that they are overpaid . . . and over here!"

Eisenhower was determined to change all that. He imposed strict discipline, instructing officers to reprimand soldiers for infractions as slight as an unpolished belt buckle. He sent GIs (American soldiers) on bus tours of London to give them an appreciation of England's history and of the price the British had already paid for their involvement in the war (many sections of London had been heavily bombed by the Germans). He banned all talk of rivalry between Americans and the British; any American soldier caught commenting about the American Army's superiority to the British armed forces was severely disciplined. And he demanded that the Americans respect the British, both as their hosts and as people who had already suffered so much for the Allied cause.

The British noticed these changes immediately, and they soon took Eisenhower into their hearts. He became almost as popular with them as their prime minister, Sir Winston Churchill. Everywhere Ike went, Londoners would wave and cheer, or stand in line to shake his hand.

Unfortunately, the British military was not as fond of Eisenhower as the public was. General Bernard Montgomery, the powerful leader of the British army, detested all Americans, and although he respected Eisenhower's "human qualities," he thought him unqualified for such an important post. However, many of England's politicians loved Eisenhower. He got along extremely well with Prime Minister Churchill, and spent many weekends at Chequers, Churchill's country estate. He also became good friends with Vice-Admiral Lord Louis Mountbatten, a high-ranking military officer and a relative of the British Royal Family. During his stay in England, Eisenhower was a regular guest at Broadlands, Mountbatten's lavish country estate.

Even King George VI liked Ike. When they met for the first time in 1942, the king explained to Eisenhower just how much he respected the American commander. The king told Ike that he remembered the day, a few weeks earlier, when Eisenhower had toured Windsor Castle. Eisenhower wondered why the king would remember the tour, especially because

Throughout the war, Eisenhower worked closely with many world leaders, including British Prime Minister Winston Churchill (left). The two men enjoyed a close friendship that lasted until Churchill's death in 1965. (Dwight D. Eisenhower Library; U.S. Army.)

the American delegation had not been presented to the Royal Family during the visit.

The king then explained. On the day that Eisenhower and his group were to visit Windsor, the constable of the palace, Lord Wigram, informed the king that there would be visitors. The king told Wigram that he and the Royal Family would remain out of sight for the day so that the tour could be conducted without any interruption. But the king forgot his promise and took his family out on the lawn for a picnic. When he saw the tour group approaching, the king suddenly remembered his promise and was horrified to think that he would embarrass Lord Wigram and his visitors. So he and the Royal Family crouched down on their hands and knees and crawled back to the palace, unseen. The farm boy from Abilene had brought the king of England to his knees!

GETTING DOWN TO BUSINESS

Creating mutual respect between Britons and Americans was an important part of Eisenhower's job in Europe, but his most vital role was as a military leader. It was his responsibility to help formulate battle strategies to defeat the Axis powers. In 1942 Eisenhower concluded that the Allies should invade North Africa, where the countries of Algeria, Morocco, and Tunisia were territories of the German-controlled French Vichy government.

But the Allies had a difficult problem to contend with in North Africa. They still considered the French as members of the Allied forces, because there were many French nationalists fighting the Nazis. But the Nazi-installed Vichy government was ruling the French territories in North Africa, and the French Army there was fighting for the Germans. The Allied purpose in North Africa was to get the Vichy French to turn against the Germans and join the Allies.

To do this, the Allies had to enlist the aid of both the French nationalists, known as the "Free French," and some Vichy commanders who secretly hated the Nazis. But many problems were involved. First of all, the Free French did not trust the British because they felt that the British had allowed the Germans to overrun France. Futhermore, the Free French despised those French leaders who had joined the Vichy government.

Eisenhower and his associates decided on a plan for the Allied invasion of North Africa, called Operation Torch. First, they would launch a major offensive. Then, after a few strategic points had been secured, they would have Vichy military leader General Henri Giraud announce to all French troops in North Africa that he was supporting the Allies. This, the Allies believed, would make the French soldiers join them in driving Hitler's army out of Africa.

Operation Torch

In early November 1942, a few days before the scheduled North African invasion, General Eisenhower flew to the Rock of Gibraltar, a small British possession on the southern coast of Spain at the entrance of the Mediterranean Sea. Gibraltar had long been an important strategic base for the British. The Rock itself was riddled with caves, which had served as secret command posts during previous British battles in the Mediterranean area. Inside these dark and humid caves, Eisenhower set up his command post. He noted in his diary that he looked forward to telling his grandchildren about how he had commanded from a cave during the war.

The day of the assault finally arrived. Eisenhower soon discovered that although the Rock was perfect for maintaining radio communications with Allied commanders in the field, there was little else he could do there except wait and see how the invasion turned out. He spent his time chain-smoking cigarettes, writing letters to Mamie, and worrying. And he had a lot to worry about. The invasion did not go as well as planned; the inroads the Allies made were few and not very important. Nevertheless, Eisenhower decided that General Giraud should go ahead and make his announcement to the French troops.

Giraud did, and the Allies waited, but nothing happened. The French troops completely ignored Giraud and continued to fight against the Allies.

The failure of the Giraud plan left Eisenhower with a bitter choice that almost ended his command of the Allied forces. There was one other Vichy leader whom the Allies felt could help them persuade the French to join their cause. His name was Admiral Jean Darlan, commander-in-chief of the Vichy forces.

The Darlan Deal

Admiral Darlan was an important cog in the Vichy machine. Responsible in large part for the French strength in North Africa, he had eagerly collaborated with Hitler, and he had helped create the Vichy government's horrible anti-Jewish laws. Nevertheless, since Giraud had been useless to the Allies, Eisenhower and others felt that only Darlan could convince the French forces in North Africa to help the Allied cause.

Darlan was hated by the British and was considered by the American press to be Hitler's puppet. Making any deal with him was sure to anger the press and the public as well. Despite this, Eisenhower decided that dealing with Darlan was a necessary evil. He instructed his deputy, Mark Clark, to negotiate with Darlan. The Allies would make Darlan High Commissioner in North Africa if he would cooperate with them. Darlan accepted, agreeing to turn the "full fury" of the French army and naval forces against Germany.

As soon as the deal was announced, Eisenhower's good

relationship with the press was over. The press accused him of collaborating with the enemy and of giving his stamp of approval to the Vichy government's undemocratic policies. Although he had realized that the decision would be an unpopular one, Ike was thoroughly unprepared for the depth of anger it aroused. Only a few days before, he had been hailed as a hero; now, he was being called a traitor.

Although the Darlan deal turned out to be a wise decision in the long run, it almost cost Eisenhower his job. The public's dismay, combined with the disappointing results of the Operation Torch assault, led to demands that Ike should go. Mamie wrote to him that "the big boys" in Washington were "preparing to give [you] the boot." When President Roosevelt and Prime Minister Churchill met in Casablanca, Morocco, for a conference in January 1943, many people believed that they would relieve Eisenhower of his command.

Roosevelt and Churchill did not fire Eisenhower, however. Both leaders realized that they were as much to blame as Eisenhower for the Darlan deal. Moreover, although Operation Torch had not succeeded thus far, they trusted Eisenhower's leadership and respected his success in getting British and American forces to work together. Eisenhower not only stayed in command, he was soon promoted to the rank of four-star general. He also learned a valuable lesson about the way politics affected military decisions.

After six months of heavy fighting, the Allies prevailed in North Africa. On May 13, 1943, the Axis forces in Tunisia surrendered. It was a costly victory—more than 10,000 Allied soldiers had lost their lives in the campaign. But the result was an important defeat for the Germans and renewed faith in the Allies' ability to fight Hitler's army. Eisenhower, for his part, experienced a renewed confidence in his own ability to command. The tide had turned once again, and Ike was once more the hero.

Care to Make a Bet?

By mid-1943 the Allies had triumphed in
Africa. Eisenhower and other Allied leaders
then turned their attention to Mussolini's
Italy. The Allies agreed that inroads had to be
made there—and soon—but they could not
agree on a strategy. They knew that any attempt to attack Italy would result in a long
and bloody battle. What they needed was to
deal a psychological blow to the morale of
Italian troops without risking thousands of Allied lives. But how?

One Italian stronghold the Allies longed to
win was the heavily fortified island of Pantelleria in the central Mediterranean Sea. But
the island was a veritable fortress; in addition
to the thousands of troops that were holding
it, the island had a rough and rocky coastline
that had earned it the name ''The Gibraltar of
the Central Mediterranean.'' Accessible only
by a narrow channel, the island was thought
to be impregnable. But Eisenhower believed
that it could be captured if it were heavily
bombarded from the air, then invaded across
the channel.

The Allied leaders argued over various
strategies, eventually adopting Eisenhower's
plan. But even after this was decided upon,
another disagreement remained. Eisenhower
believed that there were more than 11,000
Italian troops holding the island, but Prime
Minister Churchill doubted it. Churchill was
sure that there were only 3,000 Italian soldiers on the island—so sure, in fact, that he

made a bet. "If you'll give me an Italian sou for every soldier fewer than three thousand," he told Eisenhower, "I'll give you one for each man more than three thousand." The general agreed, and the bet was on.

Eisenhower's plan for capturing the island went off without a hitch. Soon after the heavy air bombardment began, white flags of surrender began to wave all over Pantelleria. Eisenhower, witnessing the surrender from a bomber flying above the island, gave the command for Allied soldiers to land, and the Italian troops were captured. When the counting was done, it was determined that almost 11,000 soldiers had been holding Pantelleria.

Needless to say, General Eisenhower won the bet, which the British prime minister gladly paid. Ike's victory was not as profitable financially as it had been strategically, however. Due to the devaluation of Italian currency during the war, Eisenhower's winnings for capturing Pantelleria came to $1.60.

Destination: Italy

Eisenhower's next big challenge was to conquer Sicily, a German-occupied island off the southern coast of Italy. Although he felt confident about the Allies' ability to take the island, Ike admitted that the day before the assault he felt "as if my stomach were a clenched fist." Once again, in a command post that was away from the action, he waited for radio reports to tell him how the invasion he had helped plan was being executed. All he could do, he wrote Mamie, was "walk, talk, try to work, smoke (all the time)," and hope things went as planned.

The Sicilian campaign resembled Operation Torch in many ways. The initial landing of Allied forces went smoothly, and thousands of Italian troops quickly surrendered. But the Germans put up such a strong resistance that the Allied gains were slow and costly. Although the Allies had 500,000 troops to the Germans' 60,000, arguments between British and American field commanders disrupted the assault, allowing the Germans to retreat from Sicily without surrendering.

Nevertheless, the Allies now had a base from which to attack the Italian mainland. Eisenhower decided to take advantage of this opportunity. And again, as in Africa, he felt that he needed the support of an enemy military commander to persuade the Italian troops to join the Allies. Although he was wary of making another Darlan deal, Ike felt once again that such a move was essential.

The leader in question this time was Marshal Pietro Badoglio, who agreed to a deal more readily than Darlan had. But at the last minute, fearing that the Allies were trying to take advantage of him, Badoglio tried to back out. Eisenhower was enraged. When Badoglio reneged on his promise to read over the radio a statement of compliance with the Allies, Eisenhower had someone else read the statement in Badoglio's name. An hour later, Badoglio repeated the statement himself. Said Ike, "[I] played a little poker" with Badoglio, and won.

OPERATION OVERLORD

After the Italian conquest, the Allies were ready for the major offensive of the war—Operation Overlord, the invasion of Europe. Beginning in Normandy, on the northwestern coast of France, it would be the greatest military operation ever attempted. And the man who led it would become one of the most important commanders in the history of warfare.

President Roosevelt and Prime Minister Churchill conducted a series of meetings and communications to decide on a leader for Operation Overlord. It was agreed that Allied unity was essential in order for the operation to be successful. No one wanted a repeat of what had happened in Sicily, when British General Bernard Montgomery and American General George S. Patton had disagreed so violently that Patton sent his troops in one direction while Montgomery sent his in another. In order for Operation Overlord to succeed in defeating Germany, it would have to be led by a strong general who had the full support of all commanders of both British and American troops.

Roosevelt at first wanted General George C. Marshall to command Operation Overlord. Marshall was the highest-ranking man in the U.S. Army—its Chief of Staff—but his duties had confined him to Washington, D.C., during the fighting. Roosevelt felt he owed it to Marshall to give him the chance to command the mission that could win the war. By late-November 1943, Eisenhower was sure that Roosevelt was going to send him to Washington to take over as the Chief of Staff and make Marshall the commander of Operation Overlord.

Eisenhower was disappointed that he would not be in charge of Overlord, but he had so much respect for Marshall that he could not really disagree with the decision. Then in December, President Roosevelt, Prime Minister Churchill, and Russian leader Josef Stalin met in Tehran, Iran, for a conference. (Stalin's Russian troops had been fighting the Germans on the Eastern Front since the war began.) In Tehran, the three leaders made a decision that would change Eisenhower's life forever—Eisenhower, not Marshall, would command Operation Overlord.

In 1943 President Franklin D. Roosevelt visited Tunis to personally inform General Eisenhower that he had been chosen to lead Operation Overlord. Until Roosevelt's visit, Eisenhower had believed that General George C. Marshall would be given the most important assignment of the war. (Dwight D. Eisenhower Library; U.S. Army.)

The reasons for choosing Eisenhower over his mentor were many. Roosevelt, who had come to rely on Marshall's constant presence in Washington, said he wouldn't be able to sleep at night with Marshall out of the country. Furthermore, Eisenhower was more popular with lower-ranking officers than was the brusk and aloof Marshall. Finally, Eisenhower had firmly demonstrated his ability to unify the troops of many nations into one solid fighting force without squabbles over national superiority.

On December 7 President Roosevelt stopped at Eisenhower's headquarters in Tunis, Tunisia, on his way back to Washington from Tehran. After a brief meeting, Eisenhower drove Roosevelt to the airport. In the car, the President turned to Eisenhower and said, "Well, Ike, you are going to command Overlord."

Eisenhower was stunned. For weeks he had been preparing to go back to Washington to assume the duties of Chief of Staff. Now, he learned that he was to lead the most important campaign of the war.

Supreme Commander

The assignment to lead Operation Overlord carried with it a title—Supreme Commander, Allied Expeditionary Force. The reality was as impressive as the title. Eisenhower was now the leader of all Allied military personnel in the war in Europe, second only to Roosevelt and Churchill in power.

Eisenhower was excited about his opportunity, but he was acutely aware of the extent of his responsibility. He would be sending thousands of soldiers from many different countries into a fierce and bloody battle. Throughout the war, he had been plagued by anger and depression over the number of young men who were being killed. He wrote to Mamie that it made him sick at heart to think of "how many youngsters are gone forever," adding, "I wish this cruel business of war could be completed quickly." He wanted to ensure that Operation Overlord was accomplished with as few Allied casualties as possible. But he also had to make sure that the invasion was successful, and that Hitler and his army were stopped once and for all.

In January 1944 Eisenhower arrived in London to assume his new post. The next six months were very exhausting because he had to coordinate every detail of the massive assault. In addition to deciding when and where the operation would take place, Ike had to decide how many troops would be deployed, who would lead them, how they would conduct their assault, and a myriad of other details. He also had to be sure that security was maintained, so that no detail of the operation leaked to the enemy.

This last task was one of Ike's most difficult. Because of the size of the assault, hundreds of officers had to be told about the plans. Naturally, when so informed, it was the only thing any of them could talk about. But those who talked too much or unwisely were severely punished. When Eisenhower learned, for example, that an American general who was also an old West Point classmate and good friend had drunk too much at a cocktail party and had mentioned the proposed date of the invasion, Ike reduced the general to the rank of colonel and sent him back to the United States. Although Ike admitted that he hated demoting officers, "particularly when they are old and warm friends," he could not allow anything to endanger the Overlord operation.

D-Day

The date set for Operation Overlord was June 5, 1944. But a few days before the invasion was to be launched, weather reports indicated that June 5 would be an overcast day. This would prevent the effective use of airplanes, which were vital to the operation's plan. Several officers recommended canceling the invasion altogether. Eisenhower alone had the authority to go ahead with the invasion or to cancel it.

Ike agonized over the decision. The day of the assault

had been precisely planned to coincide with optimal tidal conditions. If he decided to wait until tidal conditions were once again at their optimum, it would mean delaying the assault for almost two weeks. Finally, Ike made his decision: the invasion would be delayed for one day, and then, regardless of the weather, it would go ahead as planned.

In the early morning hours of June 6, 1944, the Allied forces landed on the wind-swept beaches of Normandy, just across the English Channel from England. The initial assault was successful, and the troops quickly began driving inland from the beaches. But once again, the Germans proved to be a tough fighting force. Even with the help of resistance fighters from France, the Allies were having difficulty making any major gains.

After a week, it was clear that this would be the drive that would determine the outcome of the war. It was also clear that the war on the Russian front was going to take months to resolve, and that it would be costly. Eisenhower prepared himself for a long campaign.

Two Generations of Soldiers

A week after Operation Overlord was launched Eisenhower received a visit that—temporarily, at least—revived his spirits. His son, John, who had graduated from West Point only one week earlier, had come to see his father.

Eisenhower was elated. He and John had not seen one another in two years, and Ike was bursting with pride seeing his son, now a commissioned officer in the United States Army, attired in his military dress. John, for his part, was awed by the power his father wielded; until he visited him at the front, John later commented, he had no idea how powerful a figure his father actually was.

As John was preparing to leave after his visit, he made a request. He wanted to be assigned to a fighting unit in France, where he could immediately get into battle action. His father refused him. Ike told John that giving him a special assignment would open him up to charges of favoritism. But in truth, Eisenhower's real reason was Mamie—he knew that if he sent John to the front, she would never forgive him.

Eventually, John was assigned to a communications unit; although he was now in Europe, he was not involved in any fighting. This pleased Mamie and also quelled another of Eisenhower's concerns: if John were captured at the front, the Germans would try to take advantage of having the Supreme Commander's son in their possession.

Exhaustion Takes Its Toll

By the time Operation Overlord was launched, Eisenhower had been one of the key figures in the war for more than two years. That meant two years of sleeping only four or five hours a night, of flying back and forth between continents at a moment's notice, of meeting with world leaders, and of making decisions that would ultimately affect the lives of millions of people around the world.

Eisenhower had always prided himself on his physical strength and endurance, and on his ability to remain cool under tremendous pressure. Indeed, at 53 years of age, he was an excellent specimen of a man—tall and strong, with the stamina of a man 20 years younger. But as Overlord dragged endlessly on, the constant strain, worry, and responsibility began to take its toll on Eisenhower.

Although the Allies were making gains in Europe, they were few and far between. By March 1945 Eisenhower was exhausted. He was finding it difficult to shake off common colds and other ailments. He had also reinjured the knee he had first damaged in college, and was forced at times to use a cane. Finally, at the urging of his staff officers, he agreed to take a few days off. Accompanied by a few fellow officers and some staff members, Eisenhower went to Cannes, France, to stay at a villa owned by a wealthy American.

Although he was there for four days, Eisenhower would not remember much about the luxurious villa on the French Riviera. He slept for two of the days, and spent the other two doing what he always did, talking strategy with his fellow generals. Still, he got a needed rest, and all agreed that the bags under Eisenhower's eyes had lessened somewhat by the end of the vacation.

VICTORY IN EUROPE

Had Eisenhower known what the coming months would bring, he might have taken his vacation earlier. His months of hard work, worry, and planning finally began to pay big dividends. The Germans were on the run in Europe, and on May 1 the German capital of Berlin fell to the Allies. Suddenly, less than two months after the beleaguered Supreme Commander had taken a rest to revitalize himself for the long road ahead, the war in Europe was over.

On May 7, 1945, Eisenhower himself accepted the surrender of the German army at Rhiems, France. At 2:41 A.M., Generaloberst Alfred Jodl, the German Chief of Staff, entered Eisenhower's office, where, in the presence of a small group of Allied officers and a few photographers, Eisenhower and Jodl signed the surrender agreement that forever ended the Nazi's reign of terror in Europe. VE (Victory in Europe) Day had arrived.

On May 7, 1945, General Eisenhower and British Air Marshal Arthur Tedder (right) announced to the press that the German chief of staff had signed an agreement of unconditional surrender. Although the war in the Pacific still raged, Europe was finally at peace. (Dwight D. Eisenhower Library; U.S. Army.)

Of course, World War II did not end on the same dark spring night that Hitler's empire finally toppled. There was still a war raging in the Pacific between the United States and Japan, a war that would take many more months before it came to a bloody and painful resolution. There would also be many months of clean-up work in Europe for Eisenhower and his staff. But in the early morning hours of May 7, none of that mattered. For Dwight Eisenhower, the long war was over, and it had ended in victory: victory for the Allies, for freedom, and for Eisenhower himself.

Dwight Eisenhower had taken on the biggest job in the biggest war in history, and he had made a success of it. He had made many mistakes and learned many lessons; his decisions had not always been popular, nor had they always been wise. But he had managed to defeat one of the fiercest and most determined military forces the world had ever known, and it was soundly agreed that only Eisenhower could have done it. His ability to make tough decisions, to take blame when necessary, and to create an atmosphere in which people from different backgrounds could work together for a common cause had resulted in victory. As General Marshall wrote to him, "You have completed your mission with the greatest victory in the history of warfare. . . . You have made history."

Even if Dwight Eisenhower had not been Supreme Commander of the Allied forces, he would still be remembered along with Patton, MacArthur, Marshall, and others as one of the heroes of World War II. His name would appear in history books in reference to this battle or that campaign, and historians – if not the public – would note his significance. But Eisenhower was Supreme Commander, and he lived up to that title by delivering a victory to the Allies. Because he did, he is now much more than a footnote to history – he is one of the most important figures of the 20th century.

Chapter 6
The Hero Returns

It was a warm day in New York City, and the streets were overflowing with hundreds of thousands of jubilant people. Above, thousands more peered out of open office windows, cheering and throwing streamers into the street. As an open car approached, the cheers swelled into a deafening chant: "Ike! Ike!" Dwight Eisenhower was receiving a hero's welcome.

It was July 1945, and the war in Europe was over (in the Pacific, the Japanese would surrender in August, after the atom bomb was dropped on the cities of Hiroshima and Nagasaki). Eisenhower's job in Europe was not yet finished; he would return to Germany to preside over the Allies' postwar occupation of that country. But for a few brief moments, he was basking in the glow of America's admiration.

Already, the newspapers were talking about Eisenhower running for the presidency, but nothing could have been further from his mind. He wanted, he said, to settle into a quiet life with Mamie, to hunt, to fish, to relax. He was ready to retire.

When the press and the public continued to badger him about his presidential aspirations, Eisenhower stated emphatically that he had no interest whatever in becoming President. "I cannot conceive of any set of circumstances that would drag out of me permission to consider me for any political post," he wrote. All he wanted was "to be a citizen of the United States." For the moment, the subject was closed.

LIFE WITH MAMIE

What Ike did have in mind was returning home to his wife and enjoying peace. He had been at the forefront of the great war for four years and had not seen Mamie for two. They had a lot of catching up to do. He had come back from the war a different man, and he and his wife needed a chance to get reacquainted.

In many ways, the war years had been as hard on Mamie and their marriage as they had been on Ike. She had seen her husband only once during his tour of duty in Europe, and the parting had been so difficult that she had instructed him not to come back until it was all over — she couldn't stand to say goodbye to him again. Mamie worried constantly about Ike's safety, and about the strain that his important position was putting on his health and his emotions. She also worried that she wouldn't know her husband when he finally came back to her.

Throughout their separation, the general and his wife had kept in touch through letters. Ike wrote a total of 319 letters to Mamie during the war. He wrote to quell her fears about the danger he was in and to reassure her that, despite rumors and press reports about his relationship with his female driver, he was still very much in love with her. "It's impossible for me to tell you how tremendously I miss you," he had written. Now, he wanted to show her.

But the man who returned from the war was not the same

man Mamie had married. There was now a toughness about him, a new self-assuredness, an air of command. Ike had always been very much the "boss" at home, but now it was different. He was a man who had lead one of the greatest armies ever assembled in history's biggest war. She would have to get to know him all over again.

Unfortunately, their time together would be limited. Ike first had to go back to Germany, where he headed the occupational government. When he did return home, in November 1945, it was to accept the post of Army Chief of Staff, which had been vacated by General Marshall's retirement. It was another big job—because the Army was rapidly demobilizing, Eisenhower had hundreds of details to attend to—and it left him little time for family life.

Ike and Mamie's chance to get reacquainted and to settle into a somewhat normal life came in 1948, when he accepted an appointment as president of Columbia University in New York City. On May 2, he and Mamie moved into the stately old mansion that served as the president's residence and renewed their life together. Although Ike was still a very busy man, there was now time to talk, to take trips together, and to spend time with son John, John's wife Barbara, and the Eisenhower grandchildren.

Life at Columbia

For Ike, Columbia was an education. By no standards was the new university president considered an intellectual; in fact, he had once said that "an intellectual is a man who takes more words than necessary to say more than he knows." Still, he was an organizer and a leader, and he carried with him the prestige of a conquering hero. He left most of the details of running the university to his assistants, but he became actively involved in those areas that interested him the most, particularly academic studies about world peace and foreign relations.

Although he considered the president's mansion at Columbia too ornate and stuffy for his tastes, Ike found a haven for himself in a small structure on the mansion's roof. He decorated the little shack with odds and ends of furniture and stocked it with his favorite books. Relaxing here with Mamie and friends, he felt at home for the first time in years.

DUTY CALLS AGAIN

Like every other period of rest and contentment in Eisenhower's life, his stint at Columbia University was brief. In December 1950 Ike and Mamie were in Ohio, where they had stopped on their way to visit Mamie's family in Denver. While they were waiting at a train station, an aide handed a message to Eisenhower – President Harry S. Truman wanted to speak to him immediately. Ike found a phone in the train station and called the President.

The news that Eisenhower received from Truman was another call to duty. The Allies wanted Ike to go to Europe once more, this time as Supreme European Commander of the North Atlantic Treaty Organization (NATO), a mutual defense organization that included among its members the United States, Canada, and ten Western European nations.

To a man who believed in duty as strongly as Eisenhower, there was only one answer: "Yes, Mr. President." And that is the answer Eisenhower gave to President Truman. But Ike was not thrilled with his new assignment – he had been enjoying civilian life. Nevertheless, in early 1951 he and Mamie arrived in France, where Mamie set up house and Ike set up SHAPE, the Supreme Headquarters Allied Powers Europe.

The Eisenhowers took up residence in the white-trimmed Villa St. Pierre. Mamie began a garden where she raised corn, a favorite food of Ike's that was unavailable in France. But once again, their time together was always being interrupted by the general's duties. Ike had to travel throughout Europe to meet with heads of state and military leaders, to review troops, and to study defense plans.

Once Eisenhower was back in public service, the question of his running for the presidency came up again. Opinion polls showed that a majority of Americans from both political parties would vote for him if he ran for President. Politicans representing both the Republicans and the Democrats began courting his favor. Eisenhower, who had neither belonged to nor expressed a preference for either party, dismissed the talk, insisting that he was not a politician. As he had in 1945, he thought the idea of his running for President was absurd.

In less than two years, however, Dwight Eisenhower would be elected as the 34th President of the United States. What happened? How did this man with no political aspirations suddenly become a man who first rejected — and then avidly sought — the presidency?

THE ROAD TO THE WHITE HOUSE

While Eisenhower was in France claiming no interest in entering the political arena, politicians back home were planning for the inevitable. Every stray comment that the general made in the course of his duties was placed in a political context by his supporters.

When a reporter once again asked him about which political party he belonged to, Ike said that he guessed he was a "good Kansas Republican." This was all that Republican Party leaders needed to hear. As the 1952 presidential elections approached, New York Governor Thomas E. Dewey entered Eisenhower's name in a number of state primaries. From his command post in France, Eisenhower had become a candidate for the Republican nomination for the presidency.

The results of the primaries were mixed, but they were encouraging enough for Eisenhower to take another look at his possible candidacy. He had long stated that he believed that "the voice of the people is the voice of God." Was God speaking to him? The people, it seemed, were telling him to run. He also believed that the United States—and the world—was at a crossroads, and that the nation needed an informed leader to handle the complex details of foreign policy that had emerged after the war. Was he the best man for that job?

Above all, Eisenhower believed in "that concept of duty which calls upon every good citizen to place no limitations on his readiness to serve in any designated capacity." Now, it seemed, duty was calling him to the presidency. Although previously he himself had "placed limitations" on his readiness to accept a political role, it was now time to reassess these "limitations." The people were calling, and Eisenhower had to answer them.

The Campaign Trail

On June 1, 1952, General Eisenhower was officially relieved of his duties at NATO headquarters. He retired from the military—without pay—and went on the campaign trail. The man who had once claimed that he never again wanted to hear the word "politics" was now in the thick of it.

Eisenhower, once a reluctant candidate, was a robust campaigner. As strongly as he once believed that he was not a politician, he now believed that he was the only man to lead the nation. He rallied around him the most influential members of the Republican Party, such men as Governor Dewey, Senator Henry Cabot Lodge of Massachusetts, diplomat John Foster Dulles, and Republican power-brokers J. Russell Sprague and Herbert Brownell, Jr. With their help, and with the aid of his Army-acquired organizational skills, Ike quickly built a strong campaign staff and a solid strategy.

By far Eisenhower's biggest asset in the campaign was his popularity with the public and the press. Because of his position as a great war hero, his public appearances were frequently considered "news" by the papers and the networks. Thus, he often received free air-time on television and radio, and his speeches were frequently printed in full in the daily newspapers. He used these opportunities to highlight his political agenda: reducing taxes, balancing the budget, and ending the Korean War, which had broken out in 1950.

Eisenhower's chief rival for the Republican nomination was Ohio Senator Robert Taft. The major point of contention between the two was foreign policy: Taft was an isolationist who believed that the United States should stay as much as possible out of world affairs, whereas Eisenhower's experience in the war and with NATO had led him to the conclusion that the Free World needed the United States to help it remain free.

Throughout the campaign, Eisenhower was met everywhere by cheering crowds and cries of "We Like Ike!" But at the polls, things were not so cut and dried. As the Republican National Convention approached, Eisenhower was running neck-and-neck with Taft in the all-important delegate count, which would determine the nomination. As the candidates and delegates gathered in Chicago in July 1952 for the Republican convention, no one—the press, the pollsters, nor the candidates themselves—could predict what the results would be.

The 1952 Republican National Convention

The mood was tense on the floor of Convention Hall in Chicago. The Republican Party had come to the convention with no decisive winner for its presidential nomination. The delegate count was so close that only one thing was clear—a few votes one way or the other would decide whether General Eisenhower or Senator Taft would become the Republican candidate for the presidency.

As is customary, the candidates themselves were not on the convention floor. Back in his hotel room, an exhausted Eisenhower sat in front of a television set, paying more attention to his conversation with his brother and a few assembled friends than to the convention proceedings. Finally, the first roll-call vote was cast. The results: Eisenhower 595, Taft 500. But 605 votes were needed to nominate a candidate. What would happen now?

What happened was a staple of convention politics—the switch. The delegates from Minnesota demanded attention. As a hush fell over the floor, Minnesota Senator Edward Thye shouted the news: "Minnesota wishes to change its vote to General Dwight D. Eisenhower!" The convention floor erupted in cheering: Eisenhower was over the top. The Republicans had their presidential nominee.

All that remained for Eisenhower to do was to choose his vice-presidential running mate. He selected Richard M. Nixon, a young California senator who had earned a national reputation as a member of the House Committee on Un-American Activities, which investigated possible Communist influences in the American government. When Nixon agreed to run with Eisenhower, the ticket was set, and the campaign for the White House began.

Taking It to the People

Only four months separated the Republican convention from the presidential election in November — not a lot of time to bring the Eisenhower message to the American people. When the news of his nomination reached Eisenhower's hotel room, he later related, neither he nor Mamie had any doubt that he would be the next President of the United States. The election would eventually bear out that optimism. But a few obstacles were thrown into the path of the Eisenhower campaign during the fall of 1952, and he would have to use his vast reserves of toughness and luck to overcome them and defeat the Democratic nominee, Illinois Governor Adlai Stevenson.

The first obstacle was the South. Eisenhower's staff felt that there was little use in campaigning in the southern states because they were believed to be firmly Democratic. His advisors thought that any campaigning in the South would only lead to bad press and disappointment.

Despite this advice, Eisenhower was determined to carry his campaign to the South. In September he flew to Georgia, Florida, Alabama, and Arkansas. Everywhere he went, cheering crowds greeted him; southerners clearly liked the Republican nominee. But did they like his politics; would they vote for him? Eisenhower considered the crowds a good omen, but his staff remained doubtful. Only the election results would tell the tale.

Another big problem for Eisenhower was Wisconsin Senator Joseph McCarthy, a Republican who had made a national reputation for himself by waging a campaign against suspected Communists in government. McCarthy had even gone so far as to accuse Eisenhower's good friend, General George Marshall, of being subject to Communist influence. This was clearly a dilemma for Eisenhower—he had to defend his friend and fellow officer without alienating the powerful Republican voting block that McCarthy represented.

Eisenhower would spend years defending the criticism he received over his handling of the McCarthy problem. Because he chose to defend General Marshall without attacking McCarthy or his anti-Communist mission, Democrats and liberal Republicans accused Eisenhower of buckling under to McCarthy. It was an accusation that would follow him into the White House.

The "Nixon Fund"

The greatest obstacle of Eisenhower's campaign came in mid-September, when the *New York Post* ran a front-page story about vice-presidential candidate Nixon. According to the story, Nixon had used some of the contributions he had received from wealthy Republicans to pay for personal expenses. Suddenly, papers everywhere were demanding Eisenhower's view of the "Nixon Fund."

Before Eisenhower could comment on or even get all the facts about the issue, both Democrats and Republicans were calling on him to drop Nixon from the ticket. The cornerstone of the Eisenhower campaign was honesty and morality—how could he run with an accused wrong-doer at his side?

Eisenhower was reluctant to drop Nixon, because he felt that doing so would be an admission of Nixon's guilt, and he was not convinced that Nixon was guilty. He urged calm until he could sort the problem out. Meanwhile, the chorus of protests grew stronger.

A few days after the story broke, Eisenhower's closest advisors urged him to remove Nixon from the ticket. But Nixon requested that Ike withhold his decision until Nixon could tell his side of the story directly to the people. Eisenhower agreed, and on Tuesday, September 23, Nixon went on nationwide television to explain the "secret fund."

Nixon spoke not just to the American people but also to Eisenhower. He wanted it made clear that he had no intention of bowing out gracefully, that he believed he had done no wrong, and that if he was going to leave the ticket, the Republican Party itself—not Eisenhower or his advisors—would have to ask him to do so. He ended by asking the public to "wire and write the Republican National Committee whether you think I should stay or whether you think I should get off."

Eisenhower was furious. Nixon was claiming that the committee, not the presidential candidate, should decide who the vice-presidential candidate would be. But there was no denying the effect of Nixon's speech. Congratulatory telegrams from all over the country flooded Nixon's California offices—clearly, many people had believed him. The next day, Eisenhower and Nixon met in West Virginia. "You're my boy," Eisenhower said. The crisis was over.

Election Day

On November 4, 1952, Americans went to the polls to choose the 34th President of the United States. Dwight Eisenhower could do nothing but wait. The McCarthy problem and Nixon's financial troubles had damaged the sterling reputation with which he had entered the race. How would the American people respond?

When the votes were tallied, the response was clear. Despite the many problems of the campaign, Eisenhower was the decisive winner. By what was at the time the largest margin in the history of American politics—55 percent of the popular vote—Dwight David Eisenhower was elected President of the United States. He had even carried the South.

Chapter 7

Commander-in-Chief

S tanding on a giant platform in front of the Capitol building, Dwight Eisenhower turned from Chief Justice Fred Vinson, who had just administered the presidential oath of office, to face the audience. The electric-blue eyes sparkled, and suddenly the wide, trademark grin spread across his face. As his arms shot over his head in a "V-for-Victory" sign, the people roared. It was January 20, 1953, and the largest crowd ever assembled for an American presidential inauguration was proving that the campaign slogan was true: America liked Ike.

When the cheering stopped, the reality of the moment struck Eisenhower like a thunderbolt. The poor boy from Abilene, the demerit-ridden West Point cadet, the career soldier who just over 10 years earlier was toiling in an obscure administrative post, was now the 34th President of the United States. The people liked him, there was no doubt about that. But after the applause died away, would they like Ike the President as much as they had liked Ike the war hero?

Eisenhower quickly discovered that there was little time to consider the question. As he scribbled in his diary the next evening, after his first day in the Oval Office at the White House, there were "plenty of worries and difficult problems" facing him. He had a job to do, and the best way to do it, he decided, was to plunge right in.

Eisenhower had campaigned with an ambitious platform. A few weeks before his inauguration, he met with his advisors to outline what he wanted to emphasize in his term in office. The list of tasks they compiled was daunting: ending the Korean War, continuing the policies of containment of Communism abroad and providing foreign aid to allies, reducing conventional arms strength while increasing nuclear capabilities, balancing the national budget, and reducing federal involvement in the national economy by eliminating wage and price controls. Because he intended to occupy the White House for only one term, Eisenhower had his work cut out for him.

INSIDE THE WHITE HOUSE

Before Eisenhower could start moving on any of these issues, he had to organize the White House staff and familiarize himself with the many details of government operations. An old Washington saying goes that when a new official comes to the nation's capital, "it takes [him or her] a month just to figure out where the government is." Although Eisenhower was no stranger to the Washington scene (he had lived and worked there in the 1930s while he was a member of General Marshall's staff), his party had been out of power in Washington for 20 years, and getting a Republican organization in place was no small task. He wrote in his diary on April 1 that he was constantly reminded of "how difficult it is for a party that has been in the minority for twenty years to take up the burdens of responsibility for the operation of the government."

In June 1953, President Eisenhower went on radio and television to explain his administration's programs to the public. Joining him were four members of his Cabinet, which one political analyst had called a collection of "eight millionaires and a plumber." (Dwight D. Eisenhower Library; National Park Services.)

The White House Staff

Eisenhower's technique for building his administration was taken straight from his Army experiences. The war had taught him that the Supreme Commander (and likewise, he believed, the Commander-in-Chief) could not attempt to oversee every detail himself. Therefore, Eisenhower was determined to delegate responsibilities. He assembled a Cabinet made up of some of the most noted political and business leaders in the country, such as Secretary of State John Foster Dulles, a career diplomat; Secretary of Defense Charles Wilson, the president of General Motors; and Secretary of Labor Martin Durkin, head of the American Federation of Labor's plumbers union. One newsman joked that Eisenhower had formed a Cabinet made up of "eight millionaires and a plumber," but most people agreed that the President had assembled an able staff.

While in the Army, Eisenhower had found that his chief-of-staff was invaluable in helping him oversee administrative details. As a result, he instituted the chief-of-staff system in the White House. A small army of other staffers attended to minor details so that the President could concentrate on more important issues.

In addition to those who helped him professionally, Eisenhower had a small staff of personal assistants to attend to the details of his daily living. His valet, John Moaney, had to make sure that the President didn't waste time dressing for work or state occasions. Moaney would literally dress the President: he would lay out Eisenhower's underclothing, shirt, pants, and jacket, and even help the President put his socks on and knot his tie. Although such treatment was quite regal for a boy from the Kansas plains, Eisenhower explained that he simply did not have the time to attend to such details himself.

The First Lady

The person who most helped Eisenhower adjust to life in the White House was his First Lady, Mamie. She was an exceptional hostess who enjoyed making the White House as much like a home as possible. She selected new White House china and set about redecorating the family quarters, where she and Ike spent most of their precious – and limited – time together.

One of Mamie's most notable contributions to the White House living quarters was a big double bed, which she had specially designed for herself and her husband. She had the big bed installed in the presidential bedroom. Although not all Presidents and First Ladies had shared a bedroom, Mamie said she intended to do so with Ike. She liked to reach over in the middle of the night, she explained, and "pat Ike on his old bald head anytime I want to."

Mamie used the bed as her office. She would frequently stay in it until noon, answering correspondence and making plans while her personal assistants fluttered around her. She got a lot done this way. Although some members of the White House press corps portrayed her as lazy, she was actually a very ambitious woman who admirably performed the grueling duties of a political wife, such as entertaining the wives of other leaders, hosting charity functions, and answering the thousands of letters she received from her husband's constituents.

Mamie's greatest role, however, was as friend and confidant to the President. Eisenhower sometimes felt a bit lonely on his lofty presidential perch, and it was Mamie who provided comfort and understanding. They ate dinner together almost every night in the West Sitting Hall of the White House. (When he had time, the President himself prepared the meal – one of his favorite hobbies was cooking.) After dinner, Ike would read Wild West novels or paint, while Mamie

First Lady Mamie Eisenhower posed for photographers in the gown she wore to her husband's inauguration in 1953. Mrs. Eisenhower tried to make the White House as homey as possible for her family, which had moved more than 35 times during her husband's military career. (Dwight D. Eisenhower Library.)

sat beside him, reading or writing letters. They were frequently joined for dinner by Mamie's mother, who lived with the Eisenhowers in the White House. The presence of this small but close-knit family helped Eisenhower endure the challenges that faced him daily.

A COUNTRY TO RUN

Once Eisenhower had settled his family into the White House and put his staff in order, he began tackling the problems he and his advisors had listed. Deciding which one to address first was not as difficult as Eisenhower thought it would be — outside events had a way of dictating which issues needed immediate attention. The first serious problem the new President had to face was the Korean War.

The United States had become embroiled in the Korean conflict in 1950, when Communist North Korea attacked its neighbor, South Korea. The United Nations had sent troops, most of which were Americans, to aid the South Koreans. By the time Eisenhower took office in 1953, the United States had lost thousands of soldiers in the struggle but had gained little for South Korea.

During the campaign, Eisenhower had promised that, if elected, he would go to Korea personally to assess the situation. He made good on that promise in December 1952, a month before his inauguration. Eisenhower's visit proved to him that the United States was fighting a losing battle and that the war must be ended as soon as possible. But he believed that the United States could not withdraw and leave South Korea defenseless, and he did not want to send a message to the Communists that the United States would back away and let them take over Asia. Eisenhower decided that a negotiated peace which allowed South Korea to retain its independence was the only way to end the conflict.

Eisenhower's military experience had taught him that the only way to negotiate a peace was from a position of strength. In early 1953 the United States and its ally, South Korea, were not operating from such a position. So, as he had done so frequently during World War II, Eisenhower played a little poker. He threatened the North Koreans and their Communist allies with a massive military buildup, and he even allowed Secretary of State John Foster Dulles to suggest that the United States would be willing to use nuclear weapons against the enemy if a negotiated settlement could not be reached. The gamble paid off, and on July 27, 1953, an armistice was signed. Although the war had accomplished nothing—both sides ended up almost exactly where they had been in 1950—the United States had freed itself from a bloody conflict without having to use its ultimate weapon, the atomic bomb.

Ike and the Bomb

Despite the threats he used to end the Korean War, Eisenhower had always found the thought of using nuclear weapons intolerable. In 1945 he had counseled President Truman against using the atomic bomb against Japan to end World War II (advice that Truman ignored). Eisenhower's arguments against the bomb were strategic as well as humanitarian. He not only was aware of the bomb's tremendous destructive capacity, he also knew that it would be only a matter of time before the Soviet Union acquired the knowledge to make nuclear weapons. Once that happened, Eisenhower feared that East and West would become polarized by the threat of mutual nuclear destruction.

By the time Eisenhower entered the White House, what he had once anticipated had now become a reality. The Soviets had atomic weapons and, as Eisenhower had predicted, Soviet nuclear knowledge had pushed East-West relations into a stalemate.

Determined to find a way to end the threat of nuclear war, Eisenhower made two important proposals in 1953. In April of that year, he gave his famous "Peace Speech." In it, he noted that the cost of nuclear weapons was so high that if the money were spent elsewhere, schools, hospitals, and hundreds of other peaceful projects could be undertaken. He proposed an international disarmament agreement and a universal prohibition of atomic weapons, to be supervised by the United Nations. He pledged that the United States was ready to join with other nations in forming an international fund that would use money saved by disarmament to reconstruct war-torn areas and provide other aid to needy countries.

Later that year, Eisenhower gave another famous speech on disarmament, which came to be known as the "Atoms-for-Peace" speech. On December 8, in an address to the United Nations General Assembly, Eisenhower proposed that all nations possessing nuclear capabilities—most notably, the United States and the Soviet Union—donate their stockpiles of fissionable materials to an international energy pool. Scientists could then use the materials, which the nations had been using to make nuclear bombs, to study ways of employing atomic energy for peaceful purposes. Eisenhower ended his speech by pledging that the United States would devote itself to finding "a way by which the miraculous inventiveness of man shall not be dedicated to his death, but consecrated to his life."

When Eisenhower stepped back from the microphone,

President Eisenhower spent much of his first term trying to ensure world peace. In 1954 Eisenhower's old friend, Sir Winston Churchill (second from left), visited the White House. Also pictured is U.S. Secretary of State John Foster Dulles (left), who coordinated President Eisenhower's foreign policy. (Dwight D. Eisenhower Library; National Park Services.)

the floor of the United Nations broke into wild cheering. That night, newspapers around the world proclaimed that Eisenhower had discovered the key to ending the arms race. But, as history tells us, it was not to be. Because the Soviets were skeptical of the "Atoms-for-Peace" plan, action was slow. And although the International Atomic Energy Agency that Eisenhower proposed was eventually created (in 1957), the intervening years saw both the Soviets and the Americans build up their nuclear arsenals to such an extent that the agency was all but useless.

Building a Strong Economy

Although the international scene occupied much of Eisenhower's energy during his first year in office, he also faced many domestic challenges. During the early 1950s, the population of the United States grew more rapidly than at any other time in its history. A baby boom after World War II resulted in millions of new Americans; from 1953 to 1960, the U.S. population increased by 24 million. Eisenhower faced the challenge of keeping his campaign promises to lower taxes and balance the national budget while providing jobs and housing for the country's burgeoning population.

Early analysis of the national economy proved that it would not be possible to both lower taxes and balance the budget, at least not in the first year of the Eisenhower administration. Although Republicans had long been calling for less spending on many of the social programs created during the Depression, Eisenhower did not see how a rapidly growing nation could afford drastic reductions in such programs. He decided instead that the government had to work with private industry to provide jobs, housing, and social programs.

In order to put his domestic agenda into action, Eisenhower had to win the approval of Congress. But the 82nd Congress with which the Republican Eisenhower had to deal was a Democratic one: 48 of the 96 senators and 234 of the 435 congressmen were members of the Democratic Party.

The combination of a President from one political party and a Congress largely from the opposing party has frequently led to problems on Capitol Hill. But because Eisenhower was a man skilled at uniting opposing factions, he was able to gain the trust and support of many of Congress' Democrats. As a result, the first years of his administration saw many of his domestic policies enacted.

Eisenhower's administration saw the creation of the Department of Health, Education and Welfare, designed to oversee domestic social policy. He had Congress pass a Housing Act that called for government construction of some 140,000 homes to help ease the housing shortage. He worked to expand the Social Security system, to increase the minimum wage, and to institute a highway construction program that provided thousands of jobs. He also procured funds so U.S. workers could participate in the construction of the St. Lawrence Seaway, a waterway that allows cargo ships to sail between the Atlantic Ocean and inland United States cities.

These domestic policies were such a success that by 1954 the American economy was at a postwar peak. As one Eisenhower aide noted, 1954 was "the most prosperous year that the United States ever had under a peacetime economy." By making wise reductions in defense spending, Eisenhower was able to balance the budget and to lower taxes as well. Although the nation experienced two brief periods of recession, one in the spring of 1954 and another during the winter of 1957–1958 (during Eisenhower's second term in office), Eisenhower was able to claim an inflation rate of less than one percent and a low jobless rate during his years in the White House.

The McCarthy Era

After he had been in office for a year, Eisenhower had good reason to be pleased with his accomplishments. The economy was booming, international relations were relatively peaceful, and opinion polls showed that the American people were happy with their President. But Eisenhower had been avoiding a major domestic problem, one that finally came to a head in 1954.

Eisenhower first met Wisconsin Senator Joseph McCarthy (right) on the campaign trail in 1952. After he became President, Eisenhower ignored McCarthy's hunt for Communists until the Senator destroyed himself during the Army-McCarthy hearings in 1954. (Dwight D. Eisenhower Library.)

The problem was Joseph McCarthy, the Republican senator from Wisconsin who, since 1950, had been leading a Senate investigation into Communist influences in American government. The investigation began after an American couple, Julius and Ethel Rosenberg, had been found guilty of conspiring to deliver atomic secrets to the Soviet Union. (The Rosenbergs were executed in 1953, after Eisenhower refused to invoke executive clemency to stay their executions.) The hysteria caused by the Rosenberg case fueled American fears about Communism. Soon, Americans were looking for "a Red under every bed." McCarthy, who had only recently been elected to the Senate, seized upon these fears and began to make a name for himself as the Senate's great Red hunter.

What started out in 1950 as a small campaign to protect national security had become a witch hunt by 1954. McCarthy was accusing people from every walk of life, both in and out of government, of either collaborating with the Russians or attempting to overthrow the government. With little or no evidence, he accused hundreds of Americans of being "commies," thus destroying the careers and personal lives of many individuals. So powerful had McCarthy become that even those who disagreed with his tactics, and many did, were afraid to confront him for fear of having their own reputations ruined.

Eisenhower first encountered the McCarthy problem during his presidential campaign in 1952. He decided then to avoid the issue rather than confront the senator head on. When he got to the White House, Eisenhower's policy toward McCarthy showed little change. Although he secretly loathed McCarthy, Eisenhower believed that as President he had no right to interfere with a Senate investigation. He also believed that addressing the McCarthy issue would only give credence to the senator's campaign. If he ignored McCarthy, Eisenhower thought, the senator would eventually destroy himself.

Although the technique of avoiding the McCarthy issue had worked during his first year in office, by early 1954 the press and the public were pressuring Eisenhower to do something about the senator from Wisconsin. The noted political cartoonist, Herblock, mocked the President in a cartoon that showed a timid Eisenhower, with a feather in his hand, begging a knife-wielding McCarthy to "Have a Care, Sir."

In the spring of 1954 the Senate held the infamous Army-

McCarthy hearings, in which the senator investigated Communist infiltration in what he called "the highest levels of the Armed Services." The hearings were a travesty. With no evidence to go on, McCarthy took to badgering witnesses and launching vicious attacks against those who came to defend themselves. Eisenhower's prediction came true: McCarthy destroyed himself. After watching the televised hearings, many Americans withdrew their support of McCarthy's actions. Later that year, the Senate itself censured McCarthy for his behavior during the hearings, and his career as a Communist-hunter was over.

Eisenhower and the Press

The McCarthy issue pointed up Eisenhower's major image problem during his first term in office. As the Herblock cartoon illustrated so sharply, Eisenhower was more comfortable with a feather than with a knife when facing a confrontation. Again and again, Eisenhower said his style of leadership was to quietly persuade, not to strong-arm people into accepting his viewpoint. Because of this technique, Eisenhower began facing charges that he was a weak, inactive President.

Eisenhower had always had a good relationship with the news media, and he had used it well. His 1952 presidential campaign had been the first in which television played a key role, and it had worked to Eisenhower's advantage. His good looks, quick grin, and command of the English language played right to the camera. As President, he began holding televised news conferences in 1955, and he built a closer rapport with the people by coming directly into their living rooms, much as President Roosevelt had done with his "fireside chats" over radio. Nevertheless, some members of the press were accusing Eisenhower of being a "figure-head" President.

The reason for these charges goes to the heart of who Eisenhower was as a man. First of all, he had an easy-going personality and he was honest. If a reporter asked him a question that he was unprepared for, he had no qualms about simply saying, "I don't know." Furthermore, he made no secret of the fact that he enjoyed his free time, when he could play cards, fish, or just relax with friends. Eisenhower liked to spend many of his leisure hours on the golf course, where he was usually joined by government officials with whom he would discuss business. Nevertheless, some political cartoonists portrayed him as a part-time President, playing golf while the ship of state sailed without a captain.

Overall, however, the treatment Eisenhower received from the press was similar to that of most American politicians—those who agreed with his views praised him; those from the opposing political camp did not. For the most part, Eisenhower's relationship with the press was a good one. As long as the public liked Ike, the press could do little but reflect that affection.

TOWARD A SECOND TERM

By mid-1955 the nation was already looking toward the 1956 presidential election. The question on everyone's mind: Would Eisenhower run for a second term?

Eisenhower had made it clear in 1952 that he intended to spend only one term as the country's chief executive. He had accomplished much of what he had set out to do, and

All in the Family

Political dynasties are fairly common in American politics. John Adams, America's second President, was the father of John Quincy Adams, the sixth President. Benjamin Harrison, the 23rd President, was the grandson of William Henry Harrison, the ninth President of the United States. Franklin Delano Roosevelt, who served the longest term of any U.S. President, was the cousin of Theodore Roosevelt, who served as President from 1901–1909.

Many other Presidents have been related to senators, ambassadors, and Cabinet members. John F. Kennedy, for example, was the son of the former ambassador to England. He had two brothers in politics, one of whom, Robert, served as Kennedy's Attorney General. And then there have been political marriages. Franklin Roosevelt's wife, Eleanor, was also one of Theodore Roosevelt's cousins (in fact, Theodore gave Eleanor away at her wedding to Franklin). And Theodore Roosevelt's daughter, Alice, married Nicholas Longworth, who went on to become Speaker of the House of Representatives.

Dwight Eisenhower never dreamed that he, too, would be party to the creation of a political family. Nevertheless, he was. On January 20, 1957, at his second inauguration, he introduced his grandchildren, Ann and David, to Julie and Tricia Nixon, the daughters of Vice-President Richard Nixon. Twelve years later, Julie Nixon married David Eisenhower. Once again, two American political families had joined together.

The President's grandchildren, Ann and David Eisenhower (left), met Vice-President Nixon's daughters on Inauguration Day 1957. Years later, Julie Nixon (third from left) married David Eisenhower. (Dwight D. Eisenhower Library; National Park Services.)

he was proud of his record. Furthermore, he had been at the forefront of national and international events since 1942, and he was tired. But many important matters remained unresolved—chief among them being nuclear arms control and the relationship between the United States and the Soviet Union—and Eisenhower felt deeply that the country needed someone with the strength and ability to solve them. If he decided not to run, he wondered, would the election process bring forth someone else who was adequately qualified to take up the mantle of presidential power?

Eisenhower had come to no clear answer by August 1955, when he and Mamie embarked on a trip to Denver for their annual summer vacation. The question of his candidacy was one of many issues he considered as he and Mamie made the long trip west. For the moment, however, the President was more concerned with getting in a few rounds of golf and enjoying a much-needed rest.

Pain in the Night

It was September 23, and the President wasn't having a good day on the golf course. He was playing badly, partly because he wasn't feeling well and partly because his play was constantly being interrupted by phone calls from officials in Washington. Disgusted, Eisenhower drove back to his mother-in-law's house, where he and Mamie were to spend the night. After playing a little pool with his friend George Allen, he went to bed at 10 P.M.

At around 1:30 in the morning, Mamie was awakened by the sound of her husband thrashing in his bed. "What's wrong, Ike?" she asked. The President said that he had a bad case of indigestion and asked his wife for some milk of magnesia. Mamie brought the medicine, but she became concerned when it did nothing to relieve her husband's upset. At 2 A.M., Mamie called a doctor.

When the doctor arrived, he immediately suspected that the President was suffering from more than mere indigestion. An electrocardiogram test the next morning confirmed the doctor's suspicion: the President had suffered a heart attack.

"Tell the Truth"

President Eisenhower was rushed to Fitzsimmons Army Hospital in Denver, where doctors confirmed that he had indeed suffered a heart attack. The doctors characterized the attack as "not severe, but not slight either." Although Eisenhower's chances for recovery were thought to be good, it would be a long while before he could resume the demanding duties of the presidency. Meanwhile, many questions had to be answered. Chief among them was: How much should the public be told about the President's health?

Eisenhower's response to this question was typical of the plain-spoken President. "Tell the truth, the whole truth," Eisenhower told his advisors. At the same time, he instructed that the work of the executive branch would continue; Vice-President Nixon would preside over Cabinet meetings, while the President did as much as he could from his hospital bed.

Because a heart attack is such a severe illness, many predicted that it would be months, maybe even a year, before the President regained his health. But Eisenhower and his iron constitution fooled them all. Within two weeks he was walking around his hospital room; on November 11, less than two months after his attack, Eisenhower was released from the hospital.

Surrounded by hospital personnel, President Eisenhower enjoys some sunshine a few weeks after his heart attack. An inscription on the pocket of his pajamas answered questions about his health: "Much Better Thanks." (Dwight D. Eisenhower Library; U.S. Army.)

To Run, Or Not to Run?

Before his heart attack, Eisenhower had been leaning toward announcing that he would not seek a second term. His heart attack seemed to decide the question for him. He realized, perhaps for the first time, that he was mortal. When the doctors told him that he could expect to enjoy only another 5 to 10 years of active life, Eisenhower wanted to make sure that they were years well spent.

Since 1945 Eisenhower had been dreaming of retiring to the rambling white farmhouse he owned in Gettysburg, Pennsylvania. He longed to wander about the old battlefields, hand in hand with Mamie. He also wanted to enjoy the outdoors, spend time with his family, and reflect upon his life. If he retired after the 1956 election, he could spend the rest of his days living out that long-postponed dream.

But during the weeks that Eisenhower lay in his hospital bed, another dream invaded his thoughts. This dream was of a world at peace, a world in which nuclear weapons did not loom like a spector over the globe, in which America could be strong and proud. Who would lead the country toward this dream? Alone with his thoughts, Eisenhower came back to the same belief that had led him to run for the presidency in 1952: he, and he alone, could make the dream a reality.

If he had only a few years of life left, Eisenhower decided, he should spend them serving his country. On February 29, 1957—little more than three months after he was released from the hospital—Eisenhower announced his decision to the nation: he would seek a second term as President of the United States.

Chapter 8

Four More Years

"I don't give a darn about the election!" Dwight Eisenhower thundered into the telephone. It was November 6, 1956, and Americans were going to the polls to choose their next President. But the Republican candidate had no time to worry about the returns. He was too busy being President.

The last 11 months had been some of the most difficult of Eisenhower's first term, both personally and professionally. In March he had come under attack for his civil rights policy when 101 southern congressmen called for massive resistance to the Supreme Court ruling on desegregation in the nation's schools. In June the President had been rushed to Walter Reed Hospital for emergency intestinal surgery. In October the press attacked Eisenhower for refusing to intervene when a revolution against Communist rule broke out in Hungary (the Soviet Union crushed the revolt). Now, on election day, Eisenhower's wartime allies, the British and the French, were battling Egypt over the Suez Canal, the world's largest international waterway. No wonder the President had little time to think about the election results.

Of course, it's quite possible that Eisenhower did not "give a darn" about the election because he knew he had it all sewn up. When the results were in, Eisenhower had again defeated Adlai Stevenson, the Democratic candidate – this time by an even larger margin than in 1952. As one reporter noted, "The people still 'liked Ike.' Only more so."

BACK TO WORK

There was little time for Eisenhower to celebrate this landslide, because the work of the President knows no holidays. There was a crisis at hand, and Eisenhower alone would have to handle it.

The Suez Crisis and the "Eisenhower Doctrine"

In July 1956 Gamel Abdel Nasser, the president of Egypt, seized control of the Suez Canal, which ran through his country. He also nationalized (placed under the control of the Egyptian government) the Suez Canal Company, which was largely owned by England and France. The British and French were outraged and sought the support of the United States in their dispute with the Egyptians, but Eisenhower refused to give it. He believed that the disagreement would have to be resolved in the international arena, with the help of the United Nations. The British and the French were not satisfied. On October 29 their ally, Israel, attacked Egypt, and a few days later British and French forces joined the assault.

Handling the situation was difficult for Eisenhower. He greatly respected the British and French officials who had masterminded the assault; many of them were old friends. But he felt the action their nations had taken was wrong. On October 31 Eisenhower went on national television to condemn the joint British-French-Israeli aggression and to call for an immediate end to hostilities, with a solution mandated by the United Nations. That, in the end, is just what happened. The United Nations sent an emergency force to the area, and the foreign troops withdrew.

The Suez Canal incident was later described by an Eisenhower aide as "the worst week" of Eisenhower's presidency. But out of it came one of the most important efforts of Eisenhower's administration—the "Eisenhower Doctrine." The President made agreements with many Middle Eastern nations to protect them in the event of an attack or of economic hardship. The move was designed to stop Communist influence in the area and lead to greater friendship between the United States and the Arab world.

In 1958 the Eisenhower Doctrine faced a test when the president of the small Middle East nation of Lebanon requested U.S. help in fighting a rebel movement within his country. Eisenhower sent U.S. Marines into that country and quelled the uprising. The Soviet Union did not intervene, and the Eisenhower Doctrine was hailed as a success.

The "New" Eisenhower

Eisenhower's bold moves in dealing with the Suez crisis were just the beginning of a new approach to handling the presidency that emerged during his second term. Throughout his first four years in the White House, Eisenhower had been criticized for holding back in a crisis, for waiting for problems to "solve themselves." By his second term, however, he had gained enough confidence in himself and enough knowledge of the affairs of state to be bolder and more forceful in his actions. The "new" Eisenhower did not wait to see how a crisis would resolve itself—he solved the problems through decisive action. His popularity frequently suffered in his last term because of his decisions, but he was determined to take full advantage of his role as President.

YEAR OF CRISIS

Eisenhower's decision to "get tough" came just in time, because in 1957—the first year of his second term—he would face many of the most challenging moments of his public career. Again and again he was called upon to take strong action in crises both at home and abroad.

Civil Rights

In 1957 the question of civil rights for black Americans came to the forefront of domestic politics. Although black people were guaranteed equal rights under the Constitution, many states, particularly in the South, had laws that restricted the rights of blacks to use public facilities such as buses and restrooms, to attend theaters or restaurants, and to vote in local elections. In many places, there were even separate water fountains for blacks and whites.

It was clear that such a situation could not continue. In early 1957 Eisenhower sent to Congress a Civil Rights Bill—the first such bill since the days of Reconstruction following the Civil War—that contained new measures to protect the rights of black people to vote, use public facilities, and receive justice in the legal system. The Supreme Court had ruled in 1954 that it was unconstitutional for schools to segregate students on the basis of race (many southern states had separate school systems for white and black students). The new Civil Rights Bill reinforced the idea that equal opportunity in the United States must apply to all citizens, regardless of race.

Crisis in Little Rock

In late 1957 these civil rights actions faced a grave challenge when nine black students attempted to enroll in the all-white Central High School in Little Rock, Arkansas. On the day

The issue of civil rights was one of the most controversial problems Eisenhower faced during his second term. In 1958, one year after the Little Rock school desegregation crisis, the President discussed civil rights with prominent black American leaders, including the Rev. Dr. Martin Luther King, Jr. (second from left). (Dwight D. Eisenhower Library; National Park Services.)

the black students were to enroll, a mob of white people surrounded the school, shouting racial slurs, and even beating some black men who had arrived to watch the black chidren enter. (When the black students left the school, they had to be escorted out by the police.) That same day, Arkansas Governor Orval Faubus sent National Guard troops to the school to prevent the blacks from entering.

President Eisenhower had never publicly stated his position on racial desegregation in the schools. When asked by reporters, he had always said that his job as President was to enforce Supreme Court rulings, not to comment upon them. In private, he said that he detested segregation but felt that the process of integrating black people into white institutions should proceed slowly in order to prevent violence. Now he had to act, and many people were uncertain what he would do.

The first thing Eisenhower did was to summon Governor Faubus to Newport, Rhode Island, where the President was vacationing. There, he ordered Faubus to withdraw the National Guardsmen and allow the blacks to enter, a move to which Faubus seemed to agree. But when he returned to Arkansas, Faubus commanded the troops to remain around the school. For a week, the frightened black students made no further attempts to enter.

On September 20 a federal judge ordered Governor Faubus to remove the National Guardsmen from the school. The following Monday, the black children again attempted to enter the school. This time they succeeded, but soon afterward white students began pouring out of the school. The mob of whites outside rushed toward the entrance, many threatening to kill the black children. Although local police restrained the crowd, the situation was clearly out of control. In order to prevent further violence, police once again had to escort the black students out of Central High.

It was now clear that the only person who could control

the situation in Little Rock was the President himself. At noon on September 24, 1957, Eisenhower signed an Executive Order sending federal troops to Little Rock. The 101st Airborne Division of the United States Army entered the city that night. The next day, the soldiers stood guard as the nine teenagers enrolled as the first black students at Central High. The crisis was over.

The Little Rock incident brought Eisenhower's popularity to the lowest point of his entire presidency. Southerners felt that the President had interfered with the right of a state to make its own public policy. In the North, many felt that Eisenhower's actions had come too late, that he could have stopped the violence at the outset by sending the troops sooner. But Eisenhower was not concerned. He had done what he claimed he would always do – he had enforced a ruling of the Supreme Court of the United States without regard to his personal convictions or those of some Americans. He had upheld the law.

The Space Race

Only a few days after the crisis in Little Rock ended, Eisenhower looked up to the sky and saw another problem looming. The Soviet Union had launched Sputnik I, the first man-made satellite to orbit the globe. As soon as news of the launch became public, a feeling of dread spread throughout America. The Soviet Union was clearly winning the race for new space technology. Many Americans believed that if the Soviets could create a satellite to orbit the planet, they could also create new and more powerful nuclear weapons that could rain destruction upon the United States from the sky.

The Eisenhower administration was caught completely off guard by the public reaction to the Sputnik launch. It had planned to launch its own satellite in 1957, but the plans had been shelved because other matters were considered more urgent. Now Eisenhower was being attacked in the press for not putting more effort into the American space program while the Russians forged new ground.

What the public did not know was that the Eisenhower administration had been busy with other aeronautical projects while the Soviets were working on Sputnik. The United States had developed the high-flying U-2 reconnaissance plane, which was capable of flying above Soviet radar to take clear pictures of Russian military installations. But because the U-2 project was top secret, Eisenhower could not reveal it to the public. Instead, he had to face the criticism while giving vague assurances that the United States was "well ahead" of the Soviets in the defense arena.

Meanwhile, Eisenhower sped up the U.S. satellite program. On January 31, 1958, the United States launched its own satellite, Explorer I. Although the Russians ridiculed the tiny satellite as an "orange" in comparison to the huge Sputnik, the United States was once again firmly competing in the space race.

Another Illness

On November 25, 1957, Eisenhower was sitting at his desk signing some papers when the pen suddenly fell from his hand. He tried to pick it up but found that he could not. When he looked down at the paper in front of him, he was horrified. As he later noted, "The words seemed literally to run off the top of the page." He rang for his secretary, but when she arrived he found he could not tell her what was wrong — the words that came out of his mouth were gibberish. Finding that he was able to walk, Eisenhower shambled off to bed, where he immediately fell asleep.

When he awoke, the President felt much better, and he

In December 1958 President and Mrs. Eisenhower posed for a Christmas photo with son John, daughter-in-law Barbara, and the four Eisenhower grandchildren. Only a year earlier, the President had suffered a serious stroke. (Dwight D. Eisenhower Library; National Park Services.)

believed he had suffered merely a dizzy spell. But a neuro-logical examination that afternoon revealed that he had suffered a stroke.

Of all the illnesses that Eisenhower had suffered during his term as President, this one was the most frustrating for him. The others had threatened his life, but this illness threatened his mind. For the first time, he faced the prospect of being mentally unable to carry out the duties of the presidency.

Eisenhower reacted, characteristically, with anger. When he attempted a task that he could not complete, his temper flared. He would pound his fists upon his desk in utter frustration at being unable to get his body to do what his mind commanded. But he did not give up. In the days following the stroke, he continued to go to the Oval Office, doing as much as he could before he exhausted himself. After a week or two, his condition was much improved, although he still had some difficulty speaking—he often found himself groping for a word, unable to say what his mind wanted to express.

A few weeks after his stroke, Eisenhower was scheduled to attend a NATO conference in Paris. Many aides advised against it, claiming that the strain of the high-level meeting would be too much for the President, but Eisenhower was determined to go. He believed that the conference would be the ultimate test of how complete his recovery had been. If he was unable to handle himself at the conference, he said, he would have no choice but to resign as President. Thus, when Eisenhower departed for Paris in December 1957, the future of his presidency was in doubt.

A few days after the conference began, Eisenhower drove to Marly, France, to visit NATO headquarters. When he arrived, he found a large crowd assembled expectantly in front of a microphone. His aides were visibly upset—surely a man who had just suffered a stroke could not be expected to give an unprepared speech. Nevertheless, Eisenhower walked to the microphone and began to speak. What followed stunned those who knew of the President's physical condition. For the next several minutes, Eisenhower talked nonstop about NATO and his memories of Europe during the war. Not once did he pause or grope for words. He had passed the test he had set for himself, and he had proven once and for all that he was still fit to serve as the nation's leader.

Eisenhower returned home in mid-December full of renewed optimism about himself and his country. The toughest year of his presidency had passed, and he had survived it.

Although 1957 ended on a positive note, the remaining few years of Eisenhower's term in office brought more problems. In early 1958 a recession began in the national economy, and Eisenhower found himself and his policies once more under attack (the economy improved later in the year). That summer, Eisenhower sent Marines into Lebanon as part of the Eisenhower Doctrine policy toward the Middle East, another move that sparked controversy.

The Adams Affair

Eisenhower also had to deal with a major scandal in his administration in 1958, when the House Interstate and Foreign Commerce Committee accused Sherman Adams, his chief of staff, of accepting gifts from a businessman in exchange for political favors. The committee charged that Adams had allowed a New England industrialist to pay his hotel bills and to give him expensive gifts, in return for which Adams asked the Securities and Exchange Commission (SEC) – the government agency that regulates stock dealings and other corporate business – to clear up the industrialist's tax problems.

Adams admitted accepting the gifts, but claimed that he had only asked the SEC to speed up hearings on the tax case. Nevertheless, the scandal cast a cloud over the Eisenhower administration. A congressional election was coming up in the fall of 1958, and the Republicans did not want to lose seats as a result of the scandal. Soon, Democrats and Republicans alike were calling for Adams to resign. Although Adams was a close friend, Eisenhower had no choice but to accept his resignation in September 1958.

THAWING THE COLD WAR

The most difficult problems that Eisenhower faced during his final years in office were related to the world's other super-power, the Soviet Union. When he entered office in 1953, Eisenhower was sure that he would be able to forge positive relations with the Soviet Union. He had worked closely with the Russians during World War II, when the Soviets had joined the Allies in defeating Hitler's Germany. Eisenhower knew many of the top Soviet officials personally, and he had been greeted with warmth and hospitality when he visited Russia in the late 1940s. He did not understand why the two nations had to be at odds with one another, and he wanted to do all he could to improve relations between them.

It was not an easy task. As soon as the war was over, the Soviets began expanding their influence throughout East-ern Europe. As country after country fell under communism, relations between East and West became more and more strained. By the late 1950s, a Cold War—the term used to describe a period of frosty relations between nations—was raging between the United States and the Soviet Union.

Eisenhower felt that the only way to ease tension be-tween the two superpowers was to take the case for peace to the people. He began initiating programs aimed at foster-ing goodwill between the Soviet Union and the United States. In 1959 he sent Vice-President Richard Nixon to Moscow to open the American Exhibition, a cultural fair that showed the Russian people how Americans lived. Eisenhower proposed a "People-to-People" program, in which Americans from all walks of life could meet and talk with their counterparts in other nations. And he launched the medical ship HOPE, which cruised to ports around the world bringing medical care to people in foreign countries.

A Break in the Ice

By mid-1959 Eisenhower's programs appeared to be bearing fruit. Soviet Premier Nikita Khrushchev expressed an interest in visiting the United States and in having Eisenhower visit the Soviet Union. Soon after, Eisenhower issued an official invitation to the Soviet leader. On August 5, 1959, Eisenhower announced to the world that the leader of the Soviet Union would visit the United States in mid-September.

A few weeks before Khrushchev's arrival in the United States, President Eisenhower embarked upon a tour of Europe. His purpose was twofold: to remind the Soviets just how powerful and popular the United States was in Europe, and to convince European leaders that his moves toward reconciliation with Russia would not endanger the security of America's foreign allies. The trip was an enormous success; everywhere Eisenhower went, thousands of Europeans turned out to cheer the man who had helped them defeat the Axis powers.

When he returned home on September 7, Eisenhower began making plans for the arrival of his distinguished Soviet guest. He forged an agreement with Congress to suspend all domestic squabbling between Democrats and Republicans for the duration of the premier's visit. By the time Khrushchev arrived in mid-September, a truly "united" United States was ready to greet him.

Khrushchev Comes to America

On the morning of September 15, 1959, a smiling Nikita Khrushchev stepped form his plane at Andrews Air Force Base in Washington, D.C. The Russian premier, famous for his gap-toothed grin, expected to greet another famous grinner in the President of the United States. But Eisenhower was not smiling. Almost scowling, he greeted his guest with an air of cold formality. Eisenhower was upset that the Russians had timed the launch of another space satellite to coincide with the premier's arrival, and he wanted Khrushchev to know that such propaganda ploys were not lost on the President of the United States.

After the initial chill, however, things quickly warmed up between the two leaders. Eisenhower took Khrushchev to the White House, where he was introduced to several high-ranking members of Eisenhower's Cabinet. From there, the two men boarded a helicopter for an aerial view of the nation's capital. By the time they landed, both men were smiling.

For the next 10 days, Khrushchev toured the United States with his wife and family. He visited a steel mill in Pittsburgh, where he impulsively presented a worker with his wristwatch. He traveled to Hollywood, where he posed on the lot of the Twentieth Century Fox movie studio with a number of starlets. He seemed to enjoy his tour of the country. The only problem occurred in Los Angeles, where Khrushchev got into an argument with the mayor and threatened to leave the United States and never come back. Fortunately for Eisenhower, the problem was quickly settled, and Khrushchev returned to Washington for a weekend with the President.

The two men journeyed together to Camp David, in Maryland, the presidential retreat that Eisenhower had renamed in honor of his father. (The retreat had originally been called "Shangri-la," but Eisenhower thought the name "too

*President Eisenhower and Soviet Premier Khrushchev enjoyed
a moment of laughter at Camp David in 1959, during Khrushchev's visit to the United States. Eisenhower was scheduled to
visit the Soviet Union the following year, but the Soviets withdrew the invitation after the U-2 spy plane incident in early
1960.* (Dwight D. Eisenhower Library; U.S. Navy.)

fancy" for a Kansas farm boy's weekend hideaway.) Their talks were friendly, and although no concrete agreements resulted from them, the two leaders did manage to set a date for a summit meeting between Britain, France, the United States, and Russia. They also finalized plans for Eisenhower's reciprocal visit to the Soviet Union, scheduled for early 1960.

For Eisenhower, the episode was a triumph. He had successfully played host to the leader of his nation's greatest adversary, and all had gone smoothly. When Khrushchev returned to Russia, he publicly described the President as a man sincerely working for peace. For the first time since the end of World War II, peaceful relations between the two superpowers seemed possible.

A World Traveler

Riding on the crest of his successful meeting with Khrushchev, Eisenhower set out for a tour of Europe and Asia. In December, he traveled to Italy, France, Spain, Morocco, Tunisia, Turkey, Pakistan, Afghanistan, India, Iran, and Greece. As had occurred during his trip to Europe the year before, huge crowds turned out to greet Eisenhower everywhere he went. With typical modesty, he claimed that it was not Dwight Eisenhower who the people wanted to see, but simply the President of the United States.

A few months after he returned from his triumphal tour of Europe and Asia, Eisenhower embarked upon another journey, this time to Latin America. He went to Puerto Rico, Brazil, Argentina, Chile, and Uruguay. As usual, he was warmly greeted at every stop. Workers in Brasilia, the capital of Brazil, gave him a hero's welcome. By the time Eisenhower returned home, he felt that he had gone a long way toward promoting peace and friendship between the United States and its southern neighbors.

By April 1960 Eisenhower felt that he had accomplished a lot in his second term. He had traveled around the world, spreading his message of peace. He had entertained the Soviet premier and was looking forward to meeting Khrushchev again at the Paris summit. But Eisenhower's dreams of solidifying peace between the two superpowers came to an abrupt end on May 1, 1960, when an incident over the skies of Russia shattered any hope of building a bridge of trust between the United States and the Soviet Union.

The U-2 Incident

On the afternoon of May 1, Eisenhower was in his office looking over some papers when an aide rushed in with some upsetting news. An American U-2 reconnaissance plane – the secret espionage plane that Eisenhower could not tell the public about after the Sputnik launch – had failed to return to its base after a mission over the Soviet Union. Eisenhower had to face the inevitable: the Russians had discovered the plane and shot it down.

The United States had been using U-2 planes to spy on Russian military installations since 1956. Although the planes were a secret to the public, officials in both the United States and the Soviet Union knew about them. The Soviets had not said anything because if they admitted that they knew about the flights, they would also have to admit something else – that they could not do anything to stop them. Until that bright May day, Soviet antiaircraft missiles did not have a long enough range to stop the U-2 from flying over Russia. But the Soviets had recently improved the range of their missiles, and on May 1 they were able to shoot down a U-2 near the Russian city of Sverdlovsk.

Eisenhower braced himself for a storm of criticism. It was no secret, of course, that the United States and the Soviet Union spied on one another. But wasn't it Eisenhower who had been calling for openness between the two nations? Wasn't it Eisenhower who said he wanted peace? How, then, could he justify the spying missions?

The first thing Eisenhower did was to take full responsibility for the incident. But he also did something that he hated to do, something he had sworn he would never do while in public office—he lied. Eisenhower claimed that the plane was not spying on the Soviet Union. He said that the pilot must have lost consciousness while flying the plane and had put the plane on automatic pilot, thus he "accidentally violated Soviet airspace."

Eisenhower lied about the U-2 in order to avoid an international incident. He even harbored some small hope that the Soviets would believe his story. Not only did the Soviets not believe it, they had evidence to the contrary. They had recovered debris from the plane, including a pistol, some Russian currency, and a powerful camera used to take pictures from the air. Furthermore, the plane's pilot, American serviceman Francis Gary Powers, was alive, and he was talking. In short, the Russians—and the world—knew that Eisenhower had lied.

Eisenhower now had no choice but to do what he was always most comfortable doing anyway—tell the truth. He issued a statement saying that he had authorized the espionage missions and that, furthermore, he stood behind his decision to do so. With that said, he prepared to go to the Paris summit to meet Khrushchev face to face.

The Paris Summit

When Eisenhower boarded the plane for Paris in mid-May, there were no bands playing, no crowds cheering. Usually, a President embarking on such an important international mis-

During both his terms in office, President Eisenhower took advantage of his Camp David retreat, where he could relax with wife Mamie. One of the couple's favorite pastimes was playing the "Scrabble" word game. The President, who prided himself on his vast vocabulary, frequently won at "Scrabble." (Dwight D. Eisenhower Library; U.S. Navy.)

sion would be sent off with great fanfare. But nobody felt like celebrating because the U-2 incident had cast a shadow over the entire meeting. Eisenhower boarded the plane just as he would have to face the sumit—alone.

When he sat down at his first meeting with French President Charles de Gaulle, British Prime Minister Harold Mac-Millan, and Soviet Premier Khrushchev, Eisenhower had hopes that his opening statement would ease tensions a bit. The four leaders had agreed beforehand that Eisenhower would be allowed to speak first. But de Gaulle had not even finished reading his welcoming statement when Khrushchev demanded to speak.

A flustered de Gaulle looked at Eisenhower for a reaction. The President only nodded that he had no objection.

With that, Khrushchev began his statement. Addressing himself directly to Eisenhower, he accused the United States of not really wanting peace. He further said that Eisenhower's refusal to condemn the U-2 incident had "doom[ed] the Summit Conference to complete failure in advance." He ended by withdrawing his invitation for Eisenhower to visit the Soviet Union.

Eisenhower then took the floor. He told Khrushchev that he had ordered the U-2 flights stopped, and assured him that the United States had no aggressive intentions toward the Soviet Union. But it was not enough. Khrushchev demanded that the President apologize, which Eisenhower would not do. As a result, Khrushchev and his aides walked out of the conference.

It was a glum Dwight Eisenhower who boarded the plane for his trip back to the United States. He dreaded returning home to face the barrage of questions from reporters and the decline in his popularity that the failed summit would inevitably bring. But as his plane circled the airport in preparation for landing, he looked out the window in surprise. There was a crowd below waiting to meet him.

Eisenhower had anticipated a rough return, but he hadn't expected that people would actually come to the airport to jeer him. When he stepped out of the plane, however, he was greeted by a tremendous cheer. Contrary to Eisenhower's fears, America was proud of its President. A placard placed along the road to the White House said it all: "THANK YOU, MR. PRESIDENT."

WINDING DOWN

Eisenhower was nearing the end of his term in office. Since the Constitution stipulates that a President may only serve two terms, there was no re-election campaign to plan. The

President anticipated a few peaceful final months in the White House, during which he intended to help his Vice-President, Richard Nixon, campaign for the 1960 presidential election.

Naturally, Eisenhower's last few months in office were not as peaceful as he had planned. Problems included the cancellation of his scheduled visit to Japan in the wake of anti-American riots in the capital city of Tokyo, and a volatile United Nations meeting in New York that featured Russian Premier Khrushchev banging on a desk with his shoe. But for the most part, Eisenhower concentrated on making speeches and appearances in support of Nixon, who was running against the Democratic senator from Massachusetts, John F. Kennedy.

Politics is a strange game. A politician can be extremely popular, and yet his endorsement of another candidate sometimes can mean little. This is what happened in 1960. Although the American people loved Dwight Eisenhower, his support for Nixon was not enough to sway the election in Nixon's favor. When the results came in on November 8, 1960, John F. Kennedy had become the 35th President of the United States.

The defeat was a great disappointment to Eisenhower. He was proud of the accomplishments of his presidency, and he took the Republican defeat as a rejection of his administration. As the inauguration of the new President neared, Eisenhower looked out his window at the platform being built for the ceremonies. "I feel like the fellow in jail who is watching his scaffold being built," he said sadly.

Eisenhower gave his farewell address to the American people on January 17, 1961. Considered by many historians to be one of the most significant statements of Eisenhower's presidency, the address warned that weapons manufacturers were gaining too much power over government policy. Eisenhower reminded the public that before World War II, the country had no permanent weapons industry; manufacturers who made arms during wartime returned to other manufacturing in peacetime. Since the Cold War began, however, many manufacturers had started to make nothing but weapons.

Eisenhower believed that this situation was dangerous, and he warned Americans to "guard against the acquisition of unwarranted influence, whether sought or unsought, by the military-industrial complex . . . [because] the potential for the disastrous rise of misplaced power exists and will persist." Many people believe that this message, which has become known as the "Military-Industrial Complex Speech," is as relevant today as it was in Eisenhower's day.

On January 20, 1961, Eisenhower – up to that time the oldest man to ever occupy the presidency – escorted the youngest man ever elected to that office to the inauguration ceremonies. After Kennedy had been sworn in, Eisenhower took Mamie's hand and walked to a waiting automobile. Before he entered, he waved to the assembled crowd. With that quick wave of his hand, his career as a public servant was over.

Chapter 9

Return to Abilene

For a person used to an active life, retirement can be both a blessing and a curse.

After 38 years of service to his country, Dwight Eisenhower was finally free of all military and political problems. The dream that he had long postponed — that of ambling through the countryside hand-in-hand with Mamie — had finally come true. The affairs of state were now in the hands of others. For the first time in decades, Eisenhower's life was his own.

In January 1961 the Eisenhowers returned to their white clapboard farmhouse in Gettysburg and began to live the life that had been denied them ever since their marriage 45 years before. They could now spend all their time together, without the interruption of constant crises and decisions. It was no small consolation to Mamie that, for the first time in their married life, they finally had a home of their own.

For a while, President Eisenhower enjoyed his much-needed rest. He spent many hours walking through the Gettysburg battlefield, examining the hills and dales where the great Civil War battle had been fought. He and Mamie traveled and spent time with their son and grandchildren. Ike indulged himself in his favorite hobbies, most notably cooking and oil-painting. He read the Wild West novels he so thoroughly enjoyed, and revelled in the absence of any responsibility.

In 1961, Ike and Mamie retired to their rambling farmhouse in Gettysburg, Pennsylvania, right next to the famous Civil War battlefield. It was the only home the Eisenhowers owned in their 53 years of marriage. (Dwight D. Eisenhower Library; National Park Services.)

But Eisenhower quickly became restless. There was only so much golf he could play, so many fishing trips he could take. Although he was 70 years old when he left the White House, his mind and body still craved activity. He missed being at the center of world affairs. So, as he always had, Dwight Eisenhower sought challenges.

AN ACTIVE RETIREMENT

Shortly after he left the presidency, Eisenhower told a friend, "I think I've more demands made upon me [now] than I've ever had in my life." It was not a complaint. Eisenhower was constantly searching out new endeavors, ways to keep himself involved in the world outside his comfortable Gettysburg farmhouse. Typically, he had no trouble finding them.

A Published Author

Eisenhower had written his first book before he became President. *Crusade in Europe,* published in 1948, was his personal account of the war years. After he left the White House, Eisenhower continued to write. In 1963, he published *Mandate for Change,* a book that outlined his political philosophy. Another political book, *Waging Peace,* was published in 1965. Finally, in 1967, he published a conversational and entertaining memoir entitled *At Ease: Stories I Tell to Friends.* In it, the former President shared some of his most personal memories of his childhood, Army career, and presidency.

An Elder Statesman

Eisenhower also remained active in politics after his retirement. Although no longer President, he was still the most important member of the Republican Party, frequently counseling fellow Republicans about party platforms and campaign strategies. He maintained close ties with former Vice-President Nixon, and lent his support to Nixon's successful 1968 presidential campaign.

From 1964 to 1968 Eisenhower was a close advisor to Democratic President Lyndon B. Johnson, whom he had first met during his own presidency. Although they were from opposing political parties, Johnson greatly respected Eisenhower both as a politician and as a man. He frequently called on Eisenhower for opinions and advice about pressing national and international issues. One of the most important issues that the two men discussed was the war in Vietnam, which had been brewing during Eisenhower's administration and had exploded into a full-blown conflict during the Johnson years.

A Public Man

Eisenhower remained very much in the public eye during the final years of his life. The American people loved him, and whenever he appeared to make a speech or simply to attend a function, thousands were on hand to cheer him. In 1964 millions of Americans turned on their television sets to see Eisenhower discuss his role in World War II on the program "D-Day Plus Twenty Years," hosted by newsman Walter Cronkite.

The depth of the public's affection for Eisenhower became clear in the mid- to late 1960s, when the former President's health began to decline. When Eisenhower suffered two heart attacks in 1965, messages of goodwill poured in from all over the country. These may well have helped his speedy recovery.

In April 1968 Eisenhower was felled by a fourth heart attack. A fifth followed two months later. Again cards and letters flooded the hospital. The ultimate display of affection came in August 1968, however, when Eisenhower suffered his sixth, and most severe, heart attack. More than 20 people called Walter Reed Army Hospital in Washington, D.C., to say that they would give their own hearts if a transplant would save Eisenhower's life.

The sixth attack so severely damaged Eisenhower's heart that the doctors were unsure if he would live much longer. But he once again began to show signs of a quick recovery. He was soon sitting up in bed, and was even able to go to the window to watch the hospital staff honor him with a 78th-birthday salute in October. But eventually, his body simply wore out. In late February he contracted pneumonia, and on March 28, 1969, Dwight David Eisenhower died.

FAREWELL TO A FALLEN HERO

When the news of Eisenhower's death was announced, millions of people around the world stood with bowed heads in fond memory of him. Messages of condolence poured into the United States from world leaders and ordinary citizens all over the globe. Americans flocked to churches to pray for the family of their fallen leader, President Nixon declared a national week of mourning, and flags throughout the nation were lowered to half-staff.

At the solemn funeral services in Washington, D.C., representatives of 75 foreign nations paid their respects to the man who had done so much for the world. President Nixon spoke to the thousands who had gathered to say goodbye to Dwight Eisenhower. With Mamie Eisenhower's permission, he read aloud the late President's last words: "I've always loved my country."

After the funeral services were over, Mamie Eisenhower boarded a plane for Kansas to take her husband home. He was laid to rest in Abilene, the tiny farm town where it all began.

THE EISENHOWER LEGACY

Dwight Eisenhower was a modest man. When he was in his 70s, he still referred to himself as "just a farm boy from the Kansas plains." But his record of achievement belies such a description. When he walked down that dusty Abilene street on his way to West Point in 1911, he began an odyssey that led him to the pinnacle of world leadership. He became one of the most powerful commanders in military history, and one of the most popular Presidents the United States has ever known. The farm boy became a legend.

A former West Point instructor of Eisenhower's once said: "We saw in Eisenhower a not uncommon type, a man who would thoroughly enjoy his army life . . . [but] we did not see in him a man who would throw himself into his job so completely that nothing else would matter." Over the next half-century, however, Eisenhower did indeed throw himself completely into his work. For more than 50 years, he pushed himself to the limit of physical and emotional endurance, day after day, to serve his country and his countrymen. His tireless efforts bore many fruits, and through them Dwight Eisenhower carved a permanent place for himself in the history of the United States and the world.

Bibliography

Ambrose, Stephen E. *Eisenhower the President*. New York: Simon & Schuster, 1984. Eisenhower's years in the White House are thoroughly examined by the biographer who knew him best.

Ambrose, Stephen E. *Ike: Abilene to Berlin*. New York: Harpers, 1973. Eisenhower's most respected biographer tells the story of Ike's life from his humble beginnings in a Kansas farm town to his decisive actions in the world's greatest conflict.

Eisenhower, David. *Eisenhower at War: Nineteen Forty-Three to Nineteen Forty-Five*. New York: Random House, 1986. Eisenhower's grandson takes a look at the triumphs and tragedies of Ike's tenure as commander of the Allied forces.

Eisenhower, Dwight D. *At Ease: Stories I Tell to Friends*. New York: Doubleday, 1967. In a conversational tone, Eisenhower talks about his family, his career, and his views on the world.

Eisenhower, Dwight D. *Crusade in Europe*. New York: Doubleday, 1948. Eisenhower tells his own story of the war that shaped his life and the lives of millions of people around the world.

Eisenhower, Dwight D. *The Eisenhower Diaries*. Edited by Robert H. Ferrel. New York and London: W. W. Norton, 1981. In his own words, Eisenhower records history as it is being made.

Eisenhower, Dwight D. *Waging Peace*. New York: Doubleday, 1965. Eisenhower formulates a strategy for ensuring a peaceful world.

Lyon, Peter. *Eisenhower: Portrait of the Hero.* Boston: Little, Brown, 1974. Pages of photographs and political cartoons enliven a thorough examination of Eisenhower's life and statesmanship.

Morin, Relman. *Dwight D. Eisenhower: A Gauge of Greatness.* New York: Simon & Schuster, 1969. An Associated Press reporter who covered Eisenhower's career from the Army to the White House gives an inside look at the soldier and statesman.

Slater, Ellis D. *The Ike I Knew.* New York: Ellis D. Slater Trust, 1980. One of Eisenhower's closest friends reveals what it was like to know the President during and after his term in office.

Index